Wake Up!

Traveling from good enough to great

Wendy Naarup

Copyright © 2011 Wendy Naarup
All rights reserved.

ISBN: 1461057973
ISBN-13: 9781461057970

To my parents, Wayne and Garnet Naarup, for
living lives worth emulating and for always believing in me.

Contents

Acknowledgments   vii
Prologue   ix

Part 1: Getting it wrong

CHAPTER 1
The Storm   1

CHAPTER 2
Hindsight is humbling   17

CHAPTER 3
Support   31

CHAPTER 4
Optimism   47

CHAPTER 5
You are who you hang out with   65

CHAPTER 6
If you think you can't, you can't   77

CHAPTER 7
Driving lessons   91

CHAPTER 8
Ironman   103

Part 2: Getting it right

CHAPTER 9
The spreadsheet — 117

CHAPTER 10
Your *self* — 129

CHAPTER 11
Yacht worthy — 145

CHAPTER 12
Traveling — 157

CHAPTER 13
Communication — 167

CHAPTER 14
A work in progress — 183

Epilogue — 189

Acknowledgments

"Look Mom, I did it. I closed myself in my condo for four days and wrote a book!"

I actually said that. But of course, I was wrong. It might have been four days of inspiration but it was not a book. The book happened with the help of many people who were patient enough to believe in me.

To Barbara Abramson, Steve Krawiec, Rhea Kratzer, Karen Beutler, Alan Cherkasky, Tony Free, Jeanne Loehnis, Tim Peterson, Tammy Talbot, Kimberly Martini, Mary Markman, and Kim Mittelstadt, thank you for reading one or more of the early versions and offering encouragement.

To Ken Brosky, for early copy editing, thanks to you I finally learned how to punctuate conversation.

To Mary Moran, for reading and then reading again, for lending me your dog, for keeping me organized, and especially for reminding me to open my mail, thank you.

To Judy Gaines, for reading several versions, thank you for your perspective. Your capable eyes caught everything I missed.

To Al Lautenslager, thank you for mentoring me in the world of professional speaking. You're my resource for resources.

To my daughter, Gina, and my mother, Garnet, thanks for reminiscing and patiently reading many versions. Without your input the story could not have been told.

To Calvin Husmann, for key input later in the game, thank you. You helped me keep my voice while giving me a surge of confidence.

To my dear friend Jack Reynolds, thank you for providing insight throughout the journey. You read every version, asked critical questions, and pushed me forward even when I thought I was done. You never wavered in your support of the project or of me. In the process you illustrated for me that good really isn't good enough. I'm a better writer and a better person because of your input.

To Karen Fields, thanks for the cover. Your skills with a camera are inspiring.

And finally, to my amazing support system of friends, cyclists, triathletes, and PEO sisters, you're the angels on earth who unknowingly held me up when I needed it most. Thank you. I am who I am partly because you are who you are.

Prologue

I was nineteen, heading to Florida on a thousand mile journey with my younger brother, Gary, to visit our grandmother. It was the first time we were making the trip without our parents. He did the majority of the driving but once in a while he'd get tired enough to give me a turn. Gary didn't appreciate my driving skills so he always rested with one eye open.

Suddenly, in the middle of rush hour traffic, he turned to me with an annoyed look on his face and said, "Would you please drive!"

"I am driving!" I replied, confused.

"No, you're not. You're just steering."

He was right. I was just steering, looking at scenery, day-dreaming, and barely paying attention. I was in the middle lane of a three-lane highway and cars were passing us on both sides. Maybe I was holding onto the wheel, but I wasn't driving.

I've never forgotten that comment and now recognize that the same thing happens in life. We get distracted by the scenery. It's hard to concentrate on the road with so many things going on around us. We're often pulled in conflicting directions by our families, careers, and friends, making it easy to lose sight of what we value most. If we're not careful, we find ourselves arriving somewhere, wondering how we got there and wishing we were somewhere else. The little detours we take in life aren't the problem. The problem arises when we allow a detour to become our life.

The saying goes, "Hindsight is 20/20," or "I wish I knew up front what I learned after the fact." We feel that way more often when we're "just steering" our way through life. No one lives "happily ever after" all the time, right? It's easy to look at the world around us and find circumstances far worse than our own. We're taught to be grateful for what we have. I wonder if we're content or if we're living "unhappily ever after."

To make matters worse, events happen that blindside us and knock us off course. It's as if we're driving along and suddenly find ourselves in the middle of a blizzard. Without time to react, the road turns to ice and we spin out of control, landing upside down in a ditch. I faced a personal storm of that magnitude when I was fifteen. I handled it poorly and as a result spent the next thirty-five years in life's passenger seat. I wrote *Wake Up!* because of hindsight. It's not the events in our lives that define us, it's the way we handle those events. We can't afford to spend time waiting for things to get better when we can make them better. Happiness is about finding passion and joy in the process of living. I think our lives are precious, too precious to settle for "good enough." To be effective parents, influential leaders, great students, friends or co-workers, we first have to become the best possible version of ourselves.

This book will guide you out of the storm. It will place you firmly in the driver's seat of life with your foot on the gas. Once there, you'll never let go of the wheel because life is filled with joy when you're in charge of the journey.

Part 1:
Getting it wrong

CHAPTER 1

"The soul would have no rainbow had the eyes no tears." ~JOHN VANCE CHENEY

The Storm

My coach was close by again, willing me up the final hill, reminding me to hurry. "Come on," he yelled. "You're almost there. Nice quick feet. You've got it now. This is your day. I'm proud of you."

I was trying and filled with tears again, not because of my coach or my friends and not because I was making it to the finish line. I was grateful for all of those things. I was crying because I was making it to the starting line. I was driving and I knew it. I had both hands on the wheel with the gas pedal to the floor and even though the engine was falling apart, I felt incredible. I could see. I had vision. I was in control of my life. I rounded the final turn, ran toward the finisher's chute and heard the announcer:

"From Appleton, Wisconsin, first timer, Wendy Heldt ...YOU ... ARE ... AN ... IRONMAN!!"

I crossed the tape.

It was one of those rare moments in life when everything comes together and you're better than you think you can be. My coach likes the quote, "Success happens when preparation meets opportunity." That's true, when preparation is coupled with self-esteem, determination, and heart. I learned something about the joy of accomplishment for the sake of accomplishment that day. My happiness came from within. That's not to say I didn't enjoy all the recognition for a job well done, the pats on the back and the celebrations with my circle of friends. I did. But that was the icing on the cake. Setting a goal of such magnitude, working toward that goal, overcoming obstacles along the way, then finally achieving it was priceless. I also learned that total physical exhaustion is liberating. When you're lying down, resting and can still feel your muscles working; when you're beyond tired but cannot sleep; when you're completely at peace because you put every ounce of yourself into the effort; that kind of experience is personal, emotional, and unforgettable. Ironman was a turning point. It changed my paradigm. I was no longer the girl thrown off course so many years ago by of the worst kind of storm.

✫ ✫ ✫

August 1, 1972 is a date burned in my mind forever. It was my younger brother's fourteenth birthday. We lived on a lake and my parents decided to buy him a fishing boat with an 18hp motor. It was just enough boat to have some fun with and by mid-afternoon, he'd driven the thing around enough to let me have a turn.

I was cruising down the lake when I saw someone waving to me from a dock. I slowed down to get a better look. It was Tamal, a guy few years older than me who was quite a basketball player in my town. My older brother played ball with him. Everyone knew him. Wherever he went he had an entourage of fans following close behind, but not on that day. He was standing on the end of the dock in his swimsuit with no one in sight, flagging me to bring the boat in his direction. I had a weird feeling about it. I was extremely nervous, almost sick to my stomach. Still, I felt I didn't have a good reason not to go over there. I didn't want him to think I was prejudiced.

I had witnessed plenty of racism in the three years since my family moved to the eastern shore of Maryland. But my parents taught us to see people as individuals. I played so much basketball with kids of both races that I felt immune to the problems around me. One of my closest friends was an African-American girl named Yvonne. We met in seventh grade when I accidently bumped into her standing outside the band-room door with several other students. She elbowed me back with some disgust so I returned the favor and the whole thing quickly escalated into a brawl. The sparing techniques I learned watching Dad teach my brothers how to box came in handy. I punched her as fast and as hard as I could while she scratched, clawed, and slapped me with wild intensity. We were pulled apart by other students as Mr. Adams, the band teacher, approached but not before both of us had taken a beating. Once in the room, in our respective seats, we assembled our instruments. Yvonne sat behind me in the clarinet section. I played the flute and sat in the front row.

Noticing the deep scratches on my arms, Mr. Adams asked, "Wendy is there something you'd like to tell me?"

"No, I'm fine," I replied as everyone turned to listen.

My wounds might have been obvious but I was confident that Yvonne was silently suffering behind me. Bringing a teacher into the conflict wasn't going to solve anything.

After school that day, heading to the bus, I saw Yvonne walking toward me with several of her friends. She was an impressive looking girl, nearly as tall as I but more muscular. She reminded me of a colt destined for the Triple Crown. She was full of life, a natural leader walking a step in front of her friends. I realized she wanted my attention and braced myself for the worst. Then the most amazing thing happened. She extended her hand to me.

"Damn girl, you're all right," she said, smiling. "You can fight!"

We shook hands.

"Thanks," I replied, relieved we weren't going to fight again.

Sensing my fear, she laughed and so did I. After that we became friends and played every possible sport together.

But that didn't change the fact that schools had only recently been integrated and most neighborhoods were still segregated. My neighborhood was no different. The lake was the dividing line. White kids didn't go over to the "other" side of the lake. I wanted Tamal to know I was above all of that, so in spite of my nerves, I drove the boat to the dock where he was standing. He seemed extremely happy to see me. He told me he was the lifeguard at the beach.

"Listen," he said. "The park is closed for renovations and no one's around so it's safe. Come on, I'll show you around."

This idea made me even more uncomfortable but what was I supposed to say? I couldn't come up with anything that wouldn't sound offensive to him.

"Ok," I said, slowly getting out of the boat.

I tied it to the dock and we started walking. The park was lined with trees so you couldn't see much of it from the lake. It had everything the parks on my side of the lake had except grass. It was mostly dirt and weeds but the playground equipment was great, especially the tall swings. The chains connecting the swings to the top pole must have been fifteen feet long. His park also had a lot of picnic tables and grills scattered around. I noticed some paving equipment in the parking lot which must have been the reason it was closed. It seemed odd to me that no one was around. He told me all the cool stuff was in the storage building as we walked inside. He shut the door. Because the windows were boarded up, it was pitch black. In that instant I knew I was in trouble. I started for the door but he grabbed me by the neck, lifted me up and popped my head against the concrete wall. I went from dizzy to unconscious in a matter of seconds. The next thing I remember was the horrible, rapid, panting, grunting sounds he was making and the burning pain between my legs.

"What are you doing?!" I yelled, confused. "Stop it! Please stop it! Don't do this to me!" I screamed.

I tried to hit him but he was like a crazed monster, crushing me.

I pleaded over and over and over. Then it was done. He got up and opened the door. I was on something that looked like a small surf board. He took it down by the lake and rinsed it off.

"I bet you think I'm a terrible person," he said, looking me up and down.

All I could think about was getting home. I feared for my life. I just wanted to make it back to the boat and get as far away as possible.

"No," I answered, hoping he would let me leave.

Nothing else was said as he followed me back to the boat. He stood on the dock as I tried to start the engine. I pulled the cord as hard as I could. Nothing. I pulled it again. Still nothing and I realized I was visibly shaking. He put one foot into the boat and I panicked, pulling the cord a third time. The motor started, I jammed it in reverse and pulled away from the dock.

"Come back anytime, bitch!" he yelled to me, laughing.

My mind was racing. I shouldn't have been there. I shouldn't have stopped there. What could I say to my parents? I couldn't tell them what happened. They were action people and everyone knew Tamal. The repercussions in town would have been terrible. We already had police monitoring the hallways because of racial issues at school. I thought about my older brother playing on the basketball team and what might happen to him. I was in a horrible situation and telling someone would only make matters worse. Besides, I didn't want to be *that* girl. I was precious in my father's eyes and I didn't want to change the way he looked at me. I needed a story. My head was bleeding, my shorts were ripped, and I couldn't stop shaking. What was I going to say? What was I going to do?

When I got home, no one was by the lake. I tied the boat to our dock and walked across the yard to see if anyone was around. There were no cars in the driveway. I went into the house through the side door and snuck upstairs. In the bathroom, I closed and locked the door, filled the tub and climbed in. I cried. I laid there trembling, wondering what would happen next. The whole thing was my fault. I wasn't allowed on the other side of the lake. If I just kept driving the boat none of this would have happened. I struggled to calm down but couldn't stop shaking. I let part of the water out of the tub, added a bunch of shampoo to the remaining water and turned the faucet back on. This created so many bubbles that I couldn't see myself anymore. I felt better. I didn't have to look at me. I don't remember how long I was in the tub when I heard my younger brother tapping on the door, asking me if I was OK. I got out, hid the stained shorts in back of one of my dresser drawers and never said a word.

✯ ✯ ✯

I was fifteen. The assault repeated every night in my dreams like a movie, over and over in my head. I'd wake up in the middle of it, always at the point where I regained consciousness. Sitting up, I'd realize it was a dream but the sounds he made still echoed. I did my best to cope.

I'd ride my bike to the church and climb the steps to the bell tower, push open the narrow door at the top and walk around, looking at the neighborhood below. All the houses were lined up perfectly. I imagined the parents inside with their children sharing the events of the day, none of them having a clue what had happened to me. Then I'd crouch down in a corner, wrap my arms around my legs and close my eyes so God could hold me. I had the best imagination and sometimes actually believed there were angels all around me. I prayed to them asking them to hold me so I wouldn't fall apart. I wished they would protect me at night when the dreams came. I wanted them to make the sounds go away. But they couldn't.

After a while I didn't feel whole. Have you ever been in the grocery store and dropped a piece of fruit in the produce section? If you are a considerate person, you will pick it up and put it back on the shelf. But you don't put it in your bag and take it home because it's not good anymore. That was how I saw myself. I was that piece of fruit. I was bruised on the inside and not good anymore.

I compensated by trying to be perfect. I kept my room clean. I became a straight-A student and I was even nice to my little brother. Everyone was happy with me and because they were happy with me, I felt better. The truth is, I needed everyone to be happy with me in order to feel OK. It was like a drug. My happiness became dependent on the approval of others.

Prior to the assault, I was the instigator of all things daring and constantly tested my boundaries. All through middle school, I was the kid who climbed out of classroom windows and threw paper airplanes when the teacher turned her back to write on the blackboard. I learned how to rig a sulfur match to the spring of an ink pen and would set it off while traveling between classes. The combination of smoke and smell was noxious. I was driving my way through life oblivious of any obstacles. After the assault, I stayed out of trouble and sought approval.

This new approach to life had its advantages because you can accomplish a lot when you're trying to please the right people. When I was sixteen, I started working at a drug store. I was such a responsible kid that when the pharmacist went on vacation the following year, he left me in charge. There was a guest pharmacist filling orders, but I opened and closed the store and handled the bookwork and the bank deposits. Each day I counted the money in the registers and was able to balance them to the penny, pretending it was my store. The owner was proud of me when he returned and, of course, I felt great. I was lucky because the pharmacist treated me like his daughter. He always had my best interests in mind so pleasing him was good for me.

However, this approach to life also had disadvantages. After my junior year in high school, I signed up for General Chemistry at the local college. It was a summer class and met every day. Half way through the semester, my professor was helping me with a question during lab and made a passing remark.

"You know Wendy," he said. "If you'd lose that tire around your middle, you'd be a really pretty girl."

All I heard was, "You're fat." At seventeen and still a tomboy, playing basketball with the boys, it never occurred to me that I was fat. Maybe my stomach was kind of big. I was 5'11" and weighed 145 pounds, but after that comment, I decided I weighed too much. By the time I graduated from high school, the scale showed 125 pounds. A year later, I weighed just 114 pounds.

Its amazing how one casual comment from someone I admired could have so much impact. My professor didn't realize the influence his words would have on my behavior. His comment should have gone in one ear and out the other. But it didn't. As a high school kid taking college chemistry, I looked up to him. I wanted his approval. I was just a passenger in life at this point so everything anyone said, good or bad, affected me.

A lot of people fall into this pattern for one reason or another. Maybe it's the result of parents that are more demanding than affirming. Maybe it's caused by moving to a new neighborhood and wanting to fit in. Maybe it's the by-product of a difficult relationship. Maybe it's a consequence of trying to meet everyone's expectations. Regardless of the reason, too often we judge ourselves based on the opinions of others. When we do that, we're not driving. We're letting other people set the direction for us. We feel sad, frustrated or defensive when things aren't going well because we're not in control.

As I continued to lose weight, everyone was talking about it but from my perspective I was fine. I wasn't starving myself. I was just counting calories and eating less. I would eat 800 calories a day, trying to make them as healthy as possible. My mind became a calorie calculator and I knew exactly how many I had consumed at any point in the day. I also avoided sugar and took up running. When I went to bed at night my stomach was empty and growling but in my mind it was the sound of my body chewing away at any remaining fat. I looked forward to the sensation.

One day I was in the kitchen talking to my mom while eating a giant dill pickle. We were having a fun conversation about my brilliant future when my mother completely changed the subject.

"I can't believe you're eating that, considering all the sugar it's made with."

"No way Mom," I responded, annoyed. "There isn't any sugar in a dill pickle."

"Oh yes there is," she insisted. "I watched my mother make them for years. There's tons of it in the pickling process."

Suddenly I felt ill. I couldn't take another bite and walked over to the garbage to throw it away. Then my mother dropped the bomb.

"Woops, you have a problem," she said with concern. "There really isn't any sugar in a dill pickle but just the thought of it made you feel sick. Think about it."

Think about it! All I could think about was how mad I was that she tricked me.

"So I don't like sugar. What's the crime in that?" I yelled.

"It's not the sugar that worries me," she replied. "It's your linear thinking. You used to be more flexible than that. I'm just a little concerned."

A week later, I was home again from college and my mother showed me a picture. It was a picture of me petting our German Sheppard from about a month prior. I didn't recognize myself at first.

Shocked, I thought, "Wow, who is that skinny girl! That couldn't possibly be me."

The girl in the picture was nothing but bones, long skinny bones. She looked terribly ill. That wasn't the girl I saw when I looked in the mirror. It just didn't make sense. In the mirror there was fat on my thighs. In the mirror there were places on my body where I still needed to lose weight. My image was nothing like the girl in the picture. But I knew it was me and for the first time, I acknowledged the problem. It was never my goal to hurt myself. I just wanted to be perfect. And so I learned that I could not trust my eyes alone. I had to trust the numbers on a scale and the people who cared about me. Eventually, my weight returned to 123 pounds and everyone was happy with me again so I felt OK.

During my college years, I became so accomplished at pleasing people that I turned into a chameleon of sorts, switching majors five times, each time to please a professor. I took notes in my classes in addition to notes from my text books and compiled them into study notes that I handed out to my classmates prior to exams. My goal was to make the world happy. I was good at it, so good that I didn't realize how out of control my life had become. It's not like it was spinning out of control and falling apart. On the contrary, I was accomplishing a lot but my motivation was wrong. I thought I was in charge but in reality the people I was trying to please were doing all of the driving. I was sitting in the passenger seat and would stay there until I learned to value myself from the inside out, until I learned to be centered.

It's easy to confuse "centered" with "selfish." They're not the same thing. "Selfish" means to be concerned only with yourself, to the exclusion of others. "Centered" is different. When you are in an airplane listening to the flight attendant explain the safety procedures, she always tells you to put the oxygen mask on yourself before helping someone else. Being "centered" is like that. It's about having self-esteem.

Self-esteem gives you the confidence to lead with your values. Without it your vision is impaired and the internal voice that guides you is overridden by external demands. Without self-esteem you compromise yourself into complacency and travel through life without any particular focus. That's how I got where I was at forty-five, married for the third time…because it was good for him.

CHAPTER 2

"Our greatest glory is not in never falling, but in rising every time we fall." CONFUCIUS

Hindsight is humbling

By the time I was forty-five, I was going through the motions in life. In spite of my accomplishments, there was an annoying pattern of repeated mistakes that seemed to follow me. I wasn't in charge of my happiness because I had become entrenched in the "please others" pattern. My marriage was a struggle but no one knew that. By most any standard, my life was good. It included a comfortable home, three great kids and good friends. My husband, although controlling, tried to do the right thing. My life was easy enough and I was grateful for what I had. Compared to where I'd been there was nothing to complain about. Yet no matter how hard I tried, it was an uphill battle.

One day Gina, my fifteen-year-old daughter from a previous marriage, headed outside wearing a sweatshirt instead of her winter coat. It was January and about twenty degrees in Wisconsin. We just had a foot of snow so my husband chased after her. A little while later he returned looking quite frustrated. He walked into the family room where I was playing with our sons, Matt who was five and Chad who was just three.

"Wendy, you're not going to like this," he began. I could see the regret in his eyes. "I wanted Gina to come back in to get a coat, but she said she was fine. I insisted and somehow I grabbed her and she fell into the snow. Then she started to cry and took off running. I have no idea where she went. She should have listened to me."

That was my husband. He wanted control over the things in his life, which included me, Gina and the two boys we had together. Clark was cool, calm and collected in a crisis. It was the little things in life that tripped him up. I understood his internal struggle and I cared about him so I tried to be the peacemaker, making excuses for his tone and reminding the kids how much he loved them. I also tried to give him perspective without escalating the problem.

"OK...that might have been a little over the top," I replied. "The thing about teenagers is if they get too cold, they'll come in and put more clothes on. I'm

guessing that wasn't a fight worth having in the first place."
He knew all of that but he felt compelled to defend himself. "She needs to listen to me. It's just dumb to go out there without a coat."
I let it go. There was no point arguing. In the end he would only remind me that I was too lenient with her and she'd never amount to anything. I didn't want to hear that again. Clark walked into the kitchen, back into the living room, then back into the kitchen again. He was thinking. He was obviously frustrated but needed time to process before he could talk about it and I had learned not to rush him. Everything about my husband was deliberate, even the way he paced back and forth.
"Aren't you going to look for her?" he finally asked.
"No. She's a smart girl. She has lots of friends. She'll call me in a little while and I'll go get her. We'll talk about it and everything will be OK."
"Yeah, well, she owes me an apology," he said.
I let that go, too. I wanted to tell him that maybe they could apologize to each other but I had been married to him for six years and I knew better. I also knew that he was jealous of my relationship with her.
Gina and I had a special bond. Her birth father was an abusive man. He was the product of an abusive father and struggled to find happiness in his own

life. When we met, I could see how hurt he was and I wanted to help him. I used to think I could fix people and my involvement with him turned into a turbulent relationship, a pregnancy and consequently a choice. Actually, I thought of a few choices: I could keep the pregnancy a secret from Dick and go home to my parents…I could get an abortion…I could marry him. I was living in Delaware at the time and my parents were in Wisconsin. The idea of moving far away and starting over was appealing to me so I called my mother for advice. I could tell immediately that the "illegitimate" child concept would be hard for my parents so I opted for a visit to the justice of the peace. A year and a half into that marriage, I had lost any sense of self. He owned me, controlled what I did, where I went and who I talked to. But, I had an infant I loved and was determined to protect her in the midst of it all.

When Gina was ten months old, my mother came to visit. We had moved to Florida to be closer to his parents, so the visit was a big deal. My mom was in the house spoiling her only grandchild while I ran to the grocery store. It's stifling hot in Florida in August and the drive to the grocery store was too short for the air-conditioning to cool off the car. Every short trip was like a visit to the sauna. On the way home, I couldn't wait to get back in the house. As I opened our front door with groceries in my arms, our dog slipped out. My husband erupted.

"You idiot!" he shouted. "Jesus Christ, you know the dog is always waiting at the door. God damn it, how can you be so stupid? I swear to God there's no one on the planet that's that dumb. What the hell were you thinking?"

The rant went on for twenty minutes, chasing me through the neighborhood while I called for the dog. There was no point in trying to respond as his yelling was on auto pilot.

He was so angry that he forgot about my mother. When I finally caught the dog and we returned to the house, there she was. My mother had tears in her eyes. She walked through my husband, came up to me, and put her hands on my face.

"Wendy? Are you in there?" she asked with the gentlest voice.

"Oh no, Mom, it's OK," I quickly responded. "I shouldn't have let the dog out."

Her eyes opened wider, she turned, walked back over to Dick. "You *do* realize how inappropriate your behavior was, right?"

"God, she just really pisses me off sometimes," he replied, sheepishly with his head down.

Like a mother bear protecting her cub, my mom took control of the situation. "Dick, I'm taking Wendy and Gina back to Wisconsin with me for a little break," she said. "Tomorrow we are going to pack her clothes and all of Gina's belongings and load them in the van and you're going to help. Do you understand?"

Dick was afraid of my mother. Although incredibly kind, she had the capacity to intimidate. It didn't help that she was slightly taller than him. Her confidence combined with her posture made him seem diminutive and at that moment he was completely unarmed by her presence.

"Yes," he said.

I was in awe of her strength. I was thirty years old and I was being rescued by my mother. I didn't have the tools to pull myself out of that relationship. My mother did. She was centered and consequently made it look effortless.

Driving from Florida to Wisconsin meant spending two days in the van with a ten-month-old. We made the best of it, stopping many times along the way. We talked about years gone by and about years to come, but only once did the conversation briefly turn to Dick and my current situation.

"Woops, I am so sorry that you've been living that life. Unfortunately, your father and I are too far away to understand the balance of things. We only get to see what you're willing to share. I think you've left out some important information."

"Sorry Mom, but you know the saying: As you make your bed, so you must lie in it. I'm the one who got pregnant. I'd put up with anything to raise this child. Mom, I love her so much."

"Yes, I understand and you are my little child that I love so much. As precious as Gina is to you, you are to me. Wendy, we're going to work this out. It's going to take some time, but we'll work it out."

"Thanks Mom."

That was it. My mother hoped that some distance combined with a heavy dose of family love would give me the perspective I needed to understand my predicament. It did. However, it took several weeks for me to realize that the weight of the world had been lifted from my shoulders.

Leaving an abusive relationship is like that. Many times, when you are living that life, you have no vision. Abusers isolate their victims from everyone in order to maintain their control. Still I knew the relationship wasn't normal and sometimes even threatened to leave but instead, I stayed and tried harder. Dick was nice as often as he was cruel and when he calmed down he always regretted his behavior. I was convinced that if I behaved well enough, he would stay happy. When he was angry, it was my fault. I had done something wrong. In hindsight I recognize that judging myself based on the opinions of others, not only opened the door to that relationship, it kept me locked inside.

It took space and time for me to see the extent of the mess I had gotten myself into. When I started moving forward, I never looked back knowing this was the beginning of a better life for both me and my little daughter. Gina and I spent two years with my parents before moving into our own apartment. We were a team. We talked about everything then and still do today.

Clark couldn't compete with that. Besides, Gina was eight when Clark came on the scene, and she was used to having fun. She was accustomed to using rules as guidelines. I also made sure she felt comfortable talking to me about anything. I wanted her to feel like her thoughts and ideas had value. So even around adults she expected to have a voice, to be part of the discussion and that wasn't how it worked with her stepfather. We were basically guests in his life. Over the years it had turned into "the world according to Clark." On the bright side, it was a safe place without any yelling but without any bending either. So we adjusted. The mood in the house changed to something much more serious as soon as Dad came home from work. I didn't complain about it because relatively speaking, it was ok. I was surviving my life just fine.

Gina finally called. I went to get her from a friend's house a few miles away. She came toward the car with her head down, her arms crossed, glancing up just long enough to catch the expression on my face. When I smiled at her, she relaxed and jumped in the car.

"Hey Bean, are you OK?" I asked. "You sure ran a long way."

She gave me that worried look, hoping I wasn't too disappointed.

"I'm sorry mom," she said. "Do you know what happened?"

"Yes," I said. "Dad feels pretty bad about it. It wouldn't have killed you to just come in and put on a coat, you know."

And so the conversation went. We worked it out. No harm done. She apologized to her step-father and everything was back to normal. We made it through another day. Despite recurring confrontations, this marriage offered stability to my children. As long as they were ok, I was ok. But they weren't always ok.

✪ ✪ ✪

Gina was a happy kid going into her sophomore year of high school. She was the starting setter for the varsity volleyball team and had a large group of friends. She was also getting more comfortable with the attention she received from boys. It wasn't that long ago that she'd complain about the guys who looked at her chest more than her face, not anymore. Now she was dating Patrick, a senior who had recently taken her to the homecoming dance.

Three weeks later, I was sitting on the side of her bed, rubbing her back and asking about her day when she started to cry.

"Bean, what's the matter?" I asked, stroking the side of her head.

"Patrick broke up with me Mom," she answered, crying harder.

"Honey, it's ok. It's high school. You guys haven't been going out that long. I didn't even know you liked him so much."

"Mom!" she cried, "I slept with him! And then everything started to change and now he ended it. The whole thing was probably a lie."

"Oh my god," I whispered. "Come here." I wrapped her up in a hug. "You're the most precious thing on the planet. And no, the whole thing wasn't a lie, he's just an idiot."

"I thought he really liked me Mom, I thought he loved me. But then things started changing. We were supposed to be together forever. What if he tells his friends and then people at school start finding out?"

"Ok baby, listen to me. You're still the same perfectly precious little gift to this world that you were before this happened. Do you understand that?"

"Well, not exactly. People won't think the same thing of me. Don't tell Dad and please don't tell Grandma."

"I'm not going to tell Grandma or anybody else. And don't worry about Patrick telling people either. You're only sixteen. It would be dumb for him to brag about it. But Gina, it really doesn't matter whether or not anyone knows. It doesn't change who you are. This was just one choice of thousands you're going to make. Nobody gets it right all the time."

"I hate this. It was so easy for him to walk away. How am I supposed to not feel used?"

"I don't know. You're going to feel a lot of things but you don't know what he was really thinking so try not to make assumptions. You were honest with your feelings and it didn't work out. I'm sorry it was like this but Gina, lots of boys, I should say men, are going to want your attention. Next time you'll be a little wiser."

"Mom, are you disappointed in me?" she asked, lying on her stomach again so I could continue with the back massage.

"I wish it didn't happen. I wish you were older but I'm not disappointed in you. I'm a little shocked but more than that I'm just sorry you got in over your head. How did it happen?"

"We were at his house, watching TV in his room. His parents went to bed early so it just happened. I had this big romantic idea about it but it wasn't like that. There was nothing great about it."

"Big romantic things develop from relationships that take a really long time to evolve. If a boy doesn't want to spend that time getting to know you first, it's probably not going to make you happy in the end."

"Yeah but it's different when you're in the middle of it. He said he loved me. He said a lot of things and I believed him. Mom, I thought I loved him to."

"I know, but that's the reason for taking time. You've got your whole life to have sex. Right now you're supposed to be a kid. So go to school tomorrow like nothing happened. Stay focused on your classes and your friends and eventually everything will be ok."

"Yeah, I hope you're right."

Unfortunately I wasn't right. Gina told her best girlfriend who told a few other people who told their friends and within days the news had spread throughout the school. As much as I wanted to protect her from more adversity, I couldn't.

She faced some tough challenges that year, struggling with self-esteem. I tried to help her when she'd let me but she chose to handle a lot of it on her own. However, I didn't look at the boys who knocked on our door the same anymore and I also supervised her friends more closely. I know she hated that, but I couldn't help myself. At least it gave me an idea of what was going on and occasionally it gave me an opportunity to remind her to keep looking ahead.

That year with Gina made me wish I had talked to my parents about my assault when it happened. Just like she needed support and reassurance from me, I needed it from my parents. They probably could have handled the situation. Maybe they even would have helped me without causing more problems in my community. I should have given them the chance; after all I won the parent lottery.

CHAPTER 3
---

*"To the world you may be just one person,
but to one person you may be the world."*
— JOESEPHINE BILLINGS

Support

Most parents hope and pray that their children will talk to them in a crisis. In retrospect, I wish I would have talked to mine. My parents were amazing. They were affirming, loving, fun, intelligent, forgiving, easy people. I didn't have any of those scary parent stories that so many of my friends liked to tell. Well, maybe two. There was the time my mom stuck my head in the toilet just to prove to me that I really didn't clean it. She was right.

Then there was the time my brothers and I pushed her over the edge. My mother liked a clean home. While she was cleaning the upstairs, the three of us, ages seven, eight, and nine, were in the basement making a mess. We had decided to use some old vinyl records as frisbees. By the time Mom got down there we had broken a few and she wasn't happy. We were sent to our rooms while she worked on getting the basement back into shape. Unfortunately, my older brother got a hold of Dad's shaving cream and started spraying it at us. Dad used Edge, which sprayed out like green slime. Quite a bit of it landed on the hallway carpet and we quickly discovered that it made for great sliding. The more we slid on it, the foamier it became. Pretty soon we were intentionally spraying it on the carpet and then running down the hall to see how far we could slide. We were having so much fun that we completely forgot about our mother.

I can't really explain the look on her face, but her response was calm and focused. She went into each of our rooms and packed some of our clothes in a suitcase and then she loaded us in the backseat of the car. As we drove through the surrounding neighborhoods, she'd point at a house.

"Kids! Look at that house!" she exclaimed. "I bet they like children. Wouldn't you like to live there?"

We were bawling our eyes out in the backseat.

"No mom, please take us home," we cried. "We'll be good."

She'd come to another house and repeat the offer.

"Oh kids, look at that swing set! Isn't that a nice house? I'm sure they like kids, how about that house?"

"No mom, we like our house. We'll be good!" we promised. "Please take us home!!"

Yeah, my mom was having a rough day. Even the best parents have their off days. Mine did not have many.

Childhood was a breeze in my house. My parents raised us on three simple rules:

- Treat everyone with respect.
- Do your best.
- Do the right thing just because it's the right thing to do.

Basically, that was it. If we did those things we were guaranteed to live happy lives. However, following those rules was a little more complicated than that.

Treating people with respect was straight-forward enough, however my parents were serious when they said "everyone." The kids in my small town used to tease the old man who weaved down the sidewalk. He was disabled and we thought his staggering was funny until my mom caught us laughing and mimicking him.

"Hey! What are you doing?" she scolded, acting like the world was coming to an end. "If you make fun of that, it will come and knock on your door someday."

My mom believed in Karma. She believed if you put good things out there good things would come back to you. She used to tell us that we had no right to judge a life we hadn't lived, which basically meant we couldn't judge anyone. Even when we disagreed with someone, even when someone treated us without respect, even when we were angry, we still had to be respectful. We tried.

My father didn't try to explain this rule to us, he just lived it. When I was nine he took me to his office in New York City. Dad spent nearly 40 years working for Hudson's Bay Company in Manhattan, all of those years as an executive. When we arrived, we were greeted by Joe. I was fascinated by him. His skin was the darkest shade of brown I'd ever seen, making his eyes and teeth seem unusually white. He wore a red jacket with a plaid vest, black bow-tie and black pants. He seemed important and he was clearly happy to see my father. My dad was equally happy to see him.

"Good morning, Joe!" He said as we stepped into the elevator.

"Good morning, sir," he replied, as he locked the metal cage door followed by the solid door.

"I see we have a special guest today," he added, turning his attention to me. "Hello little Miss," he grinned. "I know two things about you."

I just stared at him, waiting to see what he was going to say next.

"Your name is Wendy…and you're a very lucky little girl."

"Why?" I asked.

"Because this man is your daddy," he said pointing at my father.

Both of them chuckled. I knew they were friends. When the elevator reached the fifth floor, we got off and headed down the hall. I looked back to see if Joe was coming. He wasn't.

"Dad, where's he going?" I asked.

"Wherever someone needs him," he said.

I returned to my father's office a few more times when I was young, usually because my mother was taking us to see the department store windows during the holidays, but then we moved and ten years passed. When I was twenty, I took the train into the city again with my Dad. He'd taken a leave from his corporate job for a while, focusing time on our family mink farm. When we arrived at his office building, Joe was still there, still manning the elevator.

"Wayne!" he called out, beaming.

"Good Morning, Joe," my dad said and they hugged. "How's Janice?"

"She's much better...walking again. I see Little Miss is all grown up. Hello Ma'am," he said, bowing to me. I smiled.

"And are you a grandpa yet?" My dad asked.

"Last month, a boy, they're staying with us."

"That's great Joe! Congratulations."

As the elevator door opened my dad lingered, catching up with his friend. I was touched by their relationship. I asked my father about it later. He told me he spent thirty years going up and down that elevator four times a day with Joe.

"Of course I know him," he said.

"Yeah, but Dad, a lot of people don't do that. A lot of people pretend like Joe isn't even there."

"Not a lot of people, Woops. Some people," he said. "And it's their loss."

The respect rule was the easiest to understand. The second rule about doing your best was a little more complicated. The tricky thing about doing your best is that it's independent of everyone else and it applies to everything you do. So if we wanted to relax and do nothing, well, we were supposed to totally relax and do absolutely nothing…just revel in the nothingness. Yeah, my mom was a little over the top sometimes. If we were playing, we were supposed to play with focus, if that's even possible. And, if we were doing homework, of course we were supposed to do our best work. My younger brother struggled in school so his best work and my best work were two completely different things. However, there were no comparisons in my house. The "C's" he brought home in math were celebrated as much as the "A's" I brought home. It was always about effort. As a matter of fact, if something was easy for one of us, so easy that we could be the best without working at it, we were expected to work harder. The things that we were great at belonged in the "gifts" category. If we had a gift, we were expected to develop it.

We understood those first two rules and followed them for the most part. Of course, we were kids so the learning curve was endless. The third rule, on the other hand, gave us quite a bit of trouble. "Do the right thing just because it's the right thing to do." It sounded simple enough but it was anything but simple.

We weren't supposed to do the right thing because we wanted to go to heaven. We weren't supposed to do the right thing because we wanted our allowance. We weren't supposed to do the right thing to avoid getting punished either, but if we didn't do the right thing, we got punished. As a child this idea was confusing. For us, everything came with a reward or punishment attached. Good grades meant a bigger allowance and fighting with each other meant spending time in our bedrooms thinking about it. It just didn't make sense to do the right thing for no reason other than it was the right thing to do…that's not how the world worked.

For example, when I was in third grade, I played kickball during lunch with the boys. Most of us wore penny loafers in those days and there is no question that penny loafers were not the best playground shoes. If you kicked the ball really hard, you were likely to lose your shoe completely. Clearly, we found the flying shoe scenario extremely entertaining so one day my friends and I thought it would be fun to try to kick our shoes up onto the roof of the school. Of course, that was next to impossible for a third grader but a great activity on a warm spring day. No one could kick a shoe high enough to land it on the roof, except me. I managed to get both of mine up there...then the bell rang.

I walked into the classroom like everyone else, trying to be as discrete as possible. I even stayed close to the kids in front of me hoping their feet would hide mine. But my teacher had an eye for trouble and unfortunately, there was way too much giggling going on. She noticed.

"Wendy, where are your shoes?"

"They're on the roof," I answered.

"How did they get up there?"

At this point I knew I was in trouble and there was no way to wiggle out of it so I just confessed.

"I accidently kicked them up there."

That was all it took. She sent me to the principal's office.

The principal and I had a relationship of sorts. I was an unusually tall kid and to fit in, I tried to be funny. Often, my sense of humor landed me in his office. Fortunately for me, I was going through elementary school in the 1960s. Back then, what happened at school generally stayed at school. They rarely bothered your parents. Unfortunately for me, on this particular day the principal decided to call my mom. They had a nice chat on the phone, which seemed more than cordial to me so I wasn't too worried.

When I got home that day, I walked into the house expecting to deposit my stuff and head out to play. However, my mother had other plans. She had her hands on her hips...not a good sign.

I loved my mother's hands. Her long fingers and perfectly shaped nails were an extension of the gracefulness that represented her every movement. My mother was prettier than the other moms. People said she looked like Sophia Loren. To me she just looked like love, even when she was disappointed in my behavior.

"Slow down, young lady," she said. "You're not going anywhere today or tomorrow or the rest of the week."

Yup, I was grounded. I didn't mind the grounding so much; it was the conversation that went with it that I dreaded and I knew it was coming. She asked me a few questions about what led up to my crime and then she got down to business.

"Wendy, you're old enough to know better."

That was always the beginning.

"I'm sorry, Mom," I responded in my most obedient voice. I tried to give her that earnest look to hopefully shorten the speech but she'd had a few hours to prepare and when she continued, it was all about rule number three.

"Come on, Woops," she said. "You need to do the right thing just because it's the right thing to do and kicking your shoes up on the roof was not the right thing. The janitor had to go out there with an extension ladder to get them down. You made more work for him." She continued, "Wendy, choosing to do the right thing will make you feel good on the inside. It helps to build your character. Doing the right thing develops your moral compass and lays the groundwork for the really tough decisions you will have to make someday as an adult."

Boy, she was on a roll. My mom was great with words. She had a way of making you believe in yourself even when she was telling you how you screwed up. I was tempted to tell her that it never crossed my mind whether or not the shoe kicking idea was a right thing or a wrong thing but I decided that would only extend the conversation. And I knew what she meant. I'd heard it before…many times. She continued with examples:

"Remember when the new girl in your class walked into the classroom, tripped and dropped all of her stuff on the floor and you went over and helped her pick it up?"

"How'd you know about that?" I asked, surprised.

"I know everything," she replied, smiling.

This thought had me completely distracted. However, my mother kept talking.

"Now try to remember how that made you feel... good on the inside, right?"

"Yeah, but I had to do something. She looked like she was going to cry."

"Exactly," she said. "But no one else stepped in. When you decided to help her, you changed the rest of her day. There was no reward for you, just that good feeling. You definitely chose to do the right thing that time."

I was still thinking about whether or not she really knew everything. Then my mom surprised me.

"Sweetie, I know you were having fun and I guess I'm impressed that you managed to kick your shoes so high, but save those ideas for home, OK?"

She had that "I love you" expression on her face. The lecture was over. I was grounded for a week. That meant I had to stay inside after school and couldn't play with any of my friends. It wasn't the end of the world and as I got older I understood that third rule better. Eventually it made sense to me.

Yes, I won the parent lottery and I adored both of mine. Still, when I was fifteen I was convinced that telling them about the rape would have been a mistake. I was too worried about all the judgment that would come with it. As I got older it was hard to find a convenient time to bring it up.

Eight years later, when I was twenty-three, my mother was helping me move to Baltimore for a job with AT&T. Finally away from my home town, I spilled the story over dinner. We both cried. I could see the agony she felt over the years I struggled with the trauma on my own and regretted putting the images in her head. I convinced her I had recovered and pleaded with her to keep my secret. She agreed, except from my dad.

"Mom, you can't tell Dad!" I begged.

"Why are you so opposed to him knowing?"

"For a million reasons: Everything about the way he thinks about me will change. He wants to protect me. Remember when Marshall was working on the farm and Dad fired him because his relationship with me was too serious? God Mom, he'd be so disappointed."

"There's nothing you could ever do that would change the way your father feels about you. You are the most precious thing in the world to him and you always will be. You're going to have to trust me on this sweetheart. It's just not a secret I can keep from your dad."

She was right. Nothing changed between me and my dad, except maybe the way he gave me a hug. It seemed like he hung on just a tad longer.

I learned from sharing the story with my mom was that it's a story that's too personal to share. It was harder to talk about than I had expected and the impact it had on her was more devastating than I could have anticipated. She felt helpless and the conversation made me feel worse.

In retrospect I understand that she felt helpless because it was too late. When I chose not to tell my parents close to the time of the crisis, I paralyzed them. They couldn't fix the problem for me. They couldn't get help for me. They couldn't comfort me at night either. Those days were long gone. All they could do was love me and they were great at that.

The love and support my parents gave me turned into the love and support I gave my own children. I mirrored their example but with a different kind of radar in place because I knew how quickly things could go wrong.

In 2005, Gina graduated from high school, while Chad breezed through kindergarten. Matt, on the other hand, just survived the toughest year of his young life. He had a miserable year in second grade. We moved that year so he was the new kid in school, plus he was unusually tall so the other kids picked on him. I found myself spending a lot of time working on his confidence. His struggles reminded me of the challenges my younger brother, Gary, faced in school.

Gary was an interesting little kid. He was constantly asking questions and an answer just led to more questions. When he was five years old, our toaster broke. My father tried to fix it but eventually decided it wasn't worth the effort. Gary was right there by his shoulder the whole time and when Dad gave up, my brother got excited.

"Can I fix it, Dad?" he asked, bouncing around as if he was standing on hot coals.

"Sure. Knock yourself out," replied Dad, amused. "Just make sure you put my tools away." My father was the consummate coach and cheerleader. He'd support pretty much any idea provided it wouldn't burn down the house or cause bodily harm.

So my brother, who was not yet in kindergarten, took the toaster and the tools into his bedroom. He was in heaven. He had the entire thing apart and spread all over his bed. You would have thought it was Christmas or something, the way he played with all the parts. Several hours later, he emerged with the toaster reassembled and marched into the kitchen. He plugged it in and presto…it worked! Then he walked over to my dad and with a grin, handed him the extra parts.

From that day on, Gary was always fixing things and by the time he was in third grade, he was fixing small appliances for the garbage man. Doug and I would be playing basketball in the driveway while Gary sat on the steps in the garage with his tools and something broken, like a blender or a coffee maker. If he didn't have an appliance, he'd be fine tuning the lawn mower. He was already in control of his life, something he never relinquished.

But school was a cruel place for my little brother. He was dyslexic and back in the 60s, there weren't programs in public schools for children with learning challenges. He just had to endure and as he got older, they threw him in with all the other "problem" kids. The teasing was endless, even from my older brother and me because my mother never told us he had a problem.

I asked her about that years later and she explained, "I didn't want you to feel sorry for him. Pity wasn't going to help him in life. Plus the teasing he got from you and Doug helped me gauge the teasing he was getting at school. It allowed me to help him handle it. I always knew your brother was bright. The trick was helping him realize how bright."

Gary's middle school years were the toughest because he was so fidgety in class. Plus he was tall and skinny and had no interest in sports. He was an easy target and kids took advantage of it. The teasing turned into bullying but mom always had something for him to fix and every time he came to her rescue she reminded him how brilliant he was. In high school, he was in charge of the audio visual department and often teachers excused him from a class so he could fix some kind of technical problem. He had a gift and it gave him confidence. That confidence combined with support from my parents bolstered his self-esteem and managed to insulate my brother from the meanness around him. Gary liked the man he was becoming. He knew his life was important and that carried him past all of his difficulties.

Today he owns a manufacturing company and several patents. He's also one of the most generous people I've ever met. He's one of my heroes because he's strong from the inside out. My younger brother lives by his values, treats everyone with respect, does his best, and does the right thing just because it's the right thing to do. He's happy.

I was confident that Matt would grow past this experience too. In the same way that my mother supported Gary, I was trying to support Matt. I affirmed him at every opportunity and spent extra time each night talking with him about his day. I'd tell him how proud I was to be his mom and reinforce for him that he was a very good boy. I never missed an opportunity to reinforce the things he did well because I wanted him to believe in himself.

CHAPTER 4

"Honey, who ever told you life was fair? Besides, it will make us better people." WAYNE NAARUP

Optimism

The summer of 2005 flew by and suddenly Gina was heading off to college. I was excited for her but I also knew she would leave a huge void. She had been a big help with the boys but more than that, she was great company. Gina was a thinker. She was reflective and liked talking things through. The older she got the more fun those conversations became. The lessons she learned in high school had given her a lot of wisdom for an eighteen year old and she was a trusted resource for her friends. I was definitely going to miss my little girl.

It was the middle of August and I was about to drive her to UW-River Falls, which was four hours from home. She was a volleyball player so she was scheduled to be on campus two weeks early. This was a blessing in my mind because she'd be able to get her bearings and meet some other kids before classes started. Plus, since her roommate wouldn't be there yet, I could spend the first night with her in the dorm. That was going to be fun.

Packing for college was an experience worth remembering. Once Gina decided what she wanted to bring, I went through all of it with her and helped her cut it in half.

"No sweetheart, you really don't need to bring eight pairs of jeans," I suggested at one point.

It's amazing what that kid thought she could fit into her half of a dorm room. I promised her she could always bring more stuff later and that made her feel better. As long as Gina had options she was content. Somewhere along the way I learned to offer her a choice when I wanted to get something done. For example, when she was done packing, we still had to load the van but I knew she was tired so I gave her a choice.

"Do you want to pack up the van tonight or get up a half hour earlier tomorrow and pack it up before we leave?"

"Guess I'd rather get it done," she answered.

And we did. However, I could have handled it differently. I could have just made the decision expecting her to agree. But telling Gina what to do instead of involving her in the process would take away the sense of ownership she'd have had if I cared enough to give her a voice. We still would have gotten the job done but it probably would've sounded like this:

"Come on, let's load up the van," I could've said.

"Oh Mom, do we have to? I'm really tired," she'd whine.

"Yeah, Gina, it's not going to be any easier in the morning."

"How do you know? It might be easier in the morning."

"Fine, then I'll get you up a half hour earlier and we'll find out."

"No, that's ok. I guess we can do it now," she'd say, knowing it wasn't worth the argument. And we'd get it done, feeling grumpy the whole time.

I think most people like choices. There's no question that her effort was always better when she was part of the decision making process.

I loved traveling with my daughter. There was something about the "quality" time we had together in the car...no computer, no video games, no television, just the two of us and for most of Gina's growing-up years, no cell phones either. We didn't embrace cell phones in our family until she turned sixteen and started to drive. As she headed to college, I couldn't imagine not having that extra connection.

Gina was her usual talkative self and the four-hour drive quickly turned into a walk down memory lane. We were reminiscing about some of the conversations we'd had in the car when she was younger so I reminded her of the "birds and the bees" talk.

She was almost nine at the time and we were on our way home from a baby shower. The mom-to-be was close to her delivery date so she was showing under her shirt.

"Mom, how's that baby going to get out of there?" she asked.

Her pediatrician told me once that kids will only ask what they are ready to hear so just answer the immediate question as honestly as you can. Ok, I could handle that.

"Well, your body is kind of an amazing thing. When the baby wants to come out, his head puts pressure on the birth canal...it's kind of like a little tunnel...and it starts to get wider to make room for the baby to come out," I explained.

"Where's the birth canal?" she asked, fascinated.

Hmmm. This was getting tricky but I managed to get through that part of the discussion successfully. I was about to change the subject when she jumped in with another question.

"Mom, how'd the baby get in there in the first place?"

Oh great. It's a good thing we had an hour's drive ahead of us. I tried to keep it simple but an answer just led to another question. By the time we made it home, she understood the entire process.

At the time, the conversation exhausted me but ten years later Gina was entertained by it, until I reminded her that her brother was the same age that she was when we first talked about it.

"Oh Mom, he's too young!"

"Yeah, I think so too but the day is coming," I reminded her.

I agreed to call her when it happened. We continued with our memories for another hour and then she asked me the toughest question of the trip.

"Mom, do you really love dad?"

✡ ✡ ✡

Did I really love Clark? My mind was racing. I wanted to be careful with my answer because I recognized that this was a transitional time for her. She had a boyfriend that I wasn't excited about and she was going to be away from us for extended periods of time. I didn't want to worry her but I also didn't want her to repeat my mistakes.

"Of course I love him," I reassured her. "Why? What are you thinking about?"

"Oh, I don't know," Gina said. "I love dad and all but I don't think I want to marry someone like him. He's so stern."

"Yeah, he is, but that's mostly because of his upbringing. Eight siblings and not much money can make for lots of rules. But he means well, so I make allowances and look at the positive things." Then I added, "Dad's great in an emergency, right? And he doesn't yell much. He just needs to have control over things. You know he tries."

She was nodding her head so I continued with a story.

"Remember when you started shaving your legs and you'd be in the shower for half an hour at a time?" I asked and continued, "You should have seen your dad; steam was coming out of his ears because he was so frustrated. He'd say, 'What's she doing in there? She's killing the water bill!' Oh my God, Gina, it was hilarious. At one point, he got so mad that he lowered the hot water setting so you'd run out if you didn't hurry up. Remember that?"

"Oh yeah, I remember that." Gina laughed. "That was so mean."

"Not really, considering that Clark grew up in a house with one bathroom. Can you imagine nine kids and one bathroom? They were instructed to step into the shower, turn on the water long enough to get wet, turn off the water and suds up, and then turn the water back on long enough to rinse off. He wasn't trying to be mean; he just had a different perspective. Eventually he gave in. I told him I'd give you my shower time and I'd shower at the Y and that made him feel bad, so he lightened up on the subject. Dad isn't easy, but he's not a monster either and he cares about us."

"Yeah, I know," she agreed, "but I just don't understand why you picked him."

I struggled with her comment. She was making me think out loud.

"I hate to say it but I think it was mostly timing," I said. "I was thirty-seven and still wanted more kids. Clark wanted a family and he wanted to marry me."

That sounded pretty weak, so I tried to present a stronger front.

"He was really steady in life and I knew he had a good heart. Besides, I had Dick to compare him to and he looked pretty good in that light."

Gina wasn't satisfied. "But what about all the stuff you tell me?" she asked. "What about marrying someone who makes you love who you are in the world? What about communication? You and dad hardly ever finish a conversation."

I wasn't about to argue with her. She was right. Communication between Clark and me wasn't always reciprocal. He internalized his problems and preferred to work them out on his own. He wasn't interested in my opinion unless it supported his thinking. As for marrying someone who makes you love who you are in the world, well, that was just a dream I had for her.

"Gina, I think it's hard to get married for all the right reasons. Sometimes we get so caught up in the lives of the people who love us that we rationalize ourselves into a marriage. I did that with Dick too. He loved me and I liked feeling loved. He needed me and I liked feeling needed but those are dangerous reasons to get married. When I met Clark, I was more interested in pleasing him than thinking about myself. He was happy so I thought I was happy. I think you have to know yourself really well to make a great choice."

"But you had the best example in Grandma and Grandpa," she reminded me. "They did it right for sure. They adore each other. Grandma loves Grandpa so much and now he's not going to be around much longer."

Her tone changed.

"I can tell Mom," she said. "And Grandma will be all alone. I won't be there for her either."

Wow, talk about a subject change. I didn't see that coming.

My parents had a great marriage, night and day compared to mine. They were at fifty-one years together and counting but Gina was right, their days were numbered. My dad had Alzheimer's disease and he was well into it. It had been a gradual process for him that started about fifteen years prior, so we adjusted as he changed. He couldn't talk much anymore and he didn't know our names but he knew we belonged together and he felt safe around my mom. Unlike so many Alzheimer's patients, my father was pleasant. He was cooperative and grateful that my mom continued to care for him. He smiled at everyone not unlike a small child smiles at a friendly face. Sometimes I felt like his soul was completely exposed and we were seeing more of him than ever before.

My dad was always an easy man. He was born with a silver spoon in his mouth, but not the kind you're thinking of. No, he was not born into money. Quite the contrary, he was born in 1921 and spent most of his youth in depression-laden America. The silver spoon I'm referring to is called "optimism." My father was the younger of two children and his parents adored him. He was their golden child. His older sister by five years, on the other hand, was tall for a girl, a bit awkward, and extremely jealous of all the attention given to her younger brother. Still, she couldn't help but love him because he was naturally charming and had a way of coming out on the winning side of any challenge. My dad turned into a great looking young man with blond curly hair, blue eyes and dimples. He was an accomplished basketball player who at 6'4" went on to play in college and then semi-pro after college. However, there were some breaks in his education to serve in the war. My dad was in the Air Force during World War II. He taught pilots to fly the B25 bomber, quite a complicated process given the technology back then. He lost many close friends during the war; maybe it was that perspective that gave him so much insight in life. I always thought he had an old soul, but an old soul filled with joy. My father loved the world and the world loved him back. He never expected life to be easy but he always expected he'd be able to navigate through it successfully, and he did. Without question he was driving his way through life. He had both hands on the wheel and his foot on the gas with the confidence of an Indy driver. My dad lived a life worth emulating. One of the greatest lessons I learned from him was about optimistic thinking.

My father balanced two careers most of his life. One as an executive for Hudson's Bay Company and the other as a mink rancher. The "optimism" lesson happened on our mink farm. My dad was a geneticist by education and he cross-bred mink for color, length, and thickness of fur. In 1969 we combined our Wisconsin farm with another farm in Maryland and moved there. The thinking was that the climate made sense: Maryland winters were warmer, making it easier to keep the mink hydrated. In Wisconsin, the watering systems often froze on cold winter days. Plus Maryland was chicken producing country and chicken was one of the main ingredients in the ground-up feed that mink ate every day. He had about 40,000 mink which was a lot back then and everything was going smoothly on the new farm until the spring that the mink were exposed to botulism. Normally this wouldn't be a problem because mink are vaccinated against it; however, the baby mink (kits) are born in the spring and the new mink were too little to be vaccinated. My dad lost 30,000 mink in about three days. It was devastating but we had plenty of resources and my father restocked his farm with mink from other fur farm around the country. We continued with barely a blink. More bad news struck two years later when we discovered that some of the new mink were infected with Aleutian disease. This was a serious problem because the disease affected whelp...the number of kits a female would produce. The protocol to fix the problem was to separate the infected mink from the healthy mink and weed it out over several years. Blood samples had to be taken of every mink each year and sent to a lab in the Midwest for testing. My father was comfortable with this process. Heck, he was a scientist by education and it was easy for him to turn the farm into a lab experiment. Everything was separated. We even had different employees working on different sides of the farm. There wasn't going to be any chance of cross contamination. And again, things were progressing as expected.

 My dad used to golf with the biology professor at the local college and when they started talking about the whole scenario, the professor suggested that rather than shipping the blood samples off to a lab in the Midwest, why not just have his graduate students run the tests locally? It would save time and money and be a great project for the students. My father loved the idea, and so for the next two years everything was handled at the college. But, then he received some devastating news. The professor called my dad when he discovered that his students had been reporting the results backwards. For the past two years we had been pelting our healthy mink and keeping our infected mink. As a result, the disease had spread too far and if my dad wanted to avoid bankruptcy, he was going to have pelt out and sell the farm.

I'll never forget the conversation my parents had that night before dinner. My father was standing in the kitchen explaining the mistake to my mother. As she listened, I could see the tears building in her eyes.

"God, Wayne that is so unfair!" she said with frustration.

Remember, this was the Karma lady. My mom firmly believed that there was a balance in the universe. Doing good things, in the long run, would result in good things. This was clearly not a good thing; as a matter of fact, it was one too many bad things. But my dad was calm. He put his arms around my mother and with a consoling tone tried to put her at ease.

"Honey, who ever told you life was fair?" he asked, smiling. "Besides, it'll make us better people."

My mother pushed away, looked up at him with tears flowing.

"I don't want to be that good." she cried.

Boy, I was with her. But my dad meant it. He really didn't expect life to be fair and although he knew they were in for a couple of tough years, he also knew they'd weather the storm. He was right. My parents sold the farm and moved back to Wisconsin. They set up shop preparing other farmers' mink for auction. My mother managed the plant while my father returned to his executive position in New York. When the word got out that my parents were operating a processing plant, everyone wanted in. Turns out, the process they developed over the years on their own farm produced better looking pelts at auction so other fur farmers were excited about finally getting the same result for their mink. It was impressive. My mother worked long hard days with a crew of about 130 employees for four months of the year, while my dad flew back and forth to New York. After six years they had rebuilt a significant portion of their retirement.

And so it went with my dad's entire life. He faced a great deal of adversity but to him it was part of living. He expected it to happen, he expected the unfairness of it, he expected to handle it and most importantly, he expected to have fun. He did. My father taught us not to expect the world to be fair, but rather to move forward in the midst of the unfairness. He never settled for "good" when "great" was an option.

I now understand that he felt that way because he was centered. He understood himself from the inside out as opposed to the outside in. People didn't change him; he changed people. I think that's why he was always so happy.

But sadly, his days were numbered. Gina was right; my mom would be alone without him, painfully alone.

"Don't worry about that," I said. "Uncle Gary is right there. I'm nearby and Grandma will survive. She feels lucky to have had so many great years with him and she's had a long time to get ready. The last thing she would want is for you to worry about her when you're just starting the greatest adventure of your life, right?"

"Yeah, I know, but how long do you think he has?"

"Boy, Bean, I have no idea. Grandpa's pretty healthy in a lot of ways but I know what you are seeing. Who knows, with medicine these days, maybe he'll still be around to walk you down the aisle."

"Yeah, maybe I should hurry up and get married."

I jumped on that. "Ok, Smart Ass, you've got way too good a head on your shoulders for that."

The rest of the drive to River Falls was a breeze because the conversation never ended. And, once we got there, I could feel her excitement. We spent a few hours unloading, climbing steps, unpacking her stuff and laughing. We kept locking each other out of the room and sometimes out of the building. One time, neither of us had the card to get back in the building and we had to wait for someone else to come by. Eventually we got everything up to her room and put away. It all fit, barely, and we laughed about that too. Then we wandered around campus for several hours, went out to eat and ran into some of her teammates. Even though Gina had only met the girls once before, she greeted them warmly as if they were long lost friends. Her confidence gave me confidence in her ability to succeed on her own.

Later that night as we were lying on our twin beds, Gina started to talk about her expectations.

"I'm excited that everyone is new, that I don't have any history with anyone cuz I can re-invent myself."

"Really, who are you going to be?"

"Mom!" she exclaimed, laughing, "I'm going to be me; just a better me. In high school everyone knew all the mistakes you made and they kind of held those things against you. Going to college is like having a clean slate."

"Why am I suddenly worrying about what you did in high school that I don't know about?"

"It's not like that, Mom. It's more like boy/girl jealousy things and like rumor things that are just mean. I did some pretty dumb things in high school but nothing that you need to worry about. You already know the big stuff. I'm just thinking I'm going to make smarter decisions in college."

"I think popularity related decisions got you in the most trouble."

"Yeah, when I was younger, but that's what I'm talking about; I don't worry about that stuff anymore. The best thing you did as a parent was teach me to imagine my future. I'm getting excited about it Mom. You have nothing to worry about."

"Well, Ok then, but if you come up with something for me to worry about, promise me you'll call right away. I happen to enjoy worrying about you."

Just as I was falling asleep, I heard her whisper, "Mom? Can you tuck me in?"

I quietly got up, walked over and sat on the edge of her bed. I rubbed her back for a few minutes and then tucked the covers up under her chin and gave her a kiss on the forehead.

"Sweet dreams little girl," I whispered. "May God bless you. Let the Angels love on you."

I could tell that Gina was ready for college and I was ready to let go of her…or at least I thought I was.

I made it all the way home the next morning without shedding a tear. And then it happened. I was on the computer, catching up on e-mail, and a little box appeared on my screen. Inside were two little sentences.

"Hi Mom. How are you?"

That was it...that was the end of the facade. The tears just poured out of me. It was as if someone had turned on a faucet and I couldn't turn it off. First of all, no one had ever instant messaged me before so that was a surprise, but then, there she was. It was almost like she was sitting in my lap. I wrote a note in the little box:

"Great, but you just made me cry...how are you?"

She laughed at me and our new mode of conversation began. Even though Gina was away at college, I recognized that she would always be close to home.

CHAPTER 5

"Each friend represents a world in us, a world possibly not born until they arrive." ANÄIS NIN

You are who you hang out with

Settling Gina into college wasn't the first change I faced that year. Earlier in the year, before winter had turned to spring, Clark strongly suggested I find a job. He made it clear that he expected me to start contributing to the family income because both boys were in school and my full-time-mom status was no longer necessary. I didn't argue with him. When we met I was a bank VP. When Matt was born, I retired and apparently Clark thought I'd get tired of the stay-at-home concept. But no. I loved raising my kids and felt more than fortunate to be available when Gina reached middle school and ran into the challenges that came with puberty. It was important to me to be available to the kids but it was more important to Clark that I work. I might not have been happy about the prospect but I wanted this marriage to succeed. I knew all too well what it felt like to fail.

I was happy that I wasn't divorced. The word divorce meant failure to me and I had already failed twice. Clark was husband number three. Dick was number two. I was married to husband number one for two and a half years. We met cycling when I was twenty-five. Cycling was Larry's passion. He even worked for a bicycle distributor. Uncomfortable around women, I seemed to put him at ease. A few months after we started dating we were out on a bike ride with about twenty friends and stopped to meet someone in a field. Unbeknownst to everyone on the ride, the person we were meeting was a minister and to their shock, we exchanged vows, signed some papers and got married. I married him because he wanted to marry me. I married him because my parents wouldn't have approved if I just lived with him. I started to question the decision when he decided he didn't want children after all. I questioned it more when I realized how much our life together revolved around cycling. After a year of marriage I had five bikes. The attention was fun for a while but when I lost my nerve after a crash and didn't want to race anymore, we didn't have a foundation for anything else.

I was working for an investment company in Baltimore at the time and the owner, an intimidating, big-voiced, aggressive businessman from New Jersey, wanted me to open an office in Newark, Delaware. Mr. Cohen was a hard man. He was my father's age. He smoked cigars, invested in race cars and yelled at people...often. But when he laughed, his laughter filled a room. I was impressed with his presence and he was impressed with my attitude. He was also quick to advise me to get out of my marriage because he thought I was destined for "bigger things."

I listened. I was excited about the opportunity in Delaware but more than that I was honored that he had so much faith in me. I wanted to please him so I took the job and left Larry. I just moved out one day and never saw him again. There was no messy divorce. He filed the papers and sent me a note when it was done. For a long time I chose not to count that marriage. Clark didn't even know about it. Larry and I were more like partners than spouses anyway because both of us had issues with sex.

I was twenty-five at the time and still hadn't dealt with the assault. It was buried for the most part but sex presented some problems. The sounds Larry made were uncomfortably similar to the sounds the rapist made and they acted like triggers, making me uncomfortable. Of course this wasn't Larry's fault, so I learned to fake it. Sex turned into something I did because I should. The pattern continued in my marriage to Dick partly because of those triggers and partly because it gave me a sense of control and space in a difficult situation. I could have sex with Dick and barely be present. I decided that men really couldn't tell anyway and probably didn't care. It was something I never talked about.

A nice thing about being married to Clark was that no one had to know I was ever married before. Gina and her brothers looked alike. People just assumed she was Clark's daughter and I didn't bother to correct them. I wasn't running from my past, just ignoring it.

Everyone knows the Serenity Prayer: "God grant me the serenity to accept the things I cannot change, the courage to change the things I can, and the wisdom to know the difference." When you're lacking "centeredness," there are many things that you put into the category of "things I cannot change" and accept them. I put things into the category that I could have changed but not without a struggle and not without facing the judgment and disapproval of others.

A friend gave me the poem "The Invitation" by Oriah Mountain Dreamer. It contains this line: "I want to know if you can disappoint another to be true to yourself." I could not. At this point, I could hardly see myself. It was easy to entertain and motivate the people around me; it was easy to help others believe in themselves too, because doing those things made them happy. When I made other people happy, I felt good about myself. Optimism was my middle name. Maybe I couldn't "please all the people all the time," but I was willing to try.

Once the pattern of pleasing other people to feel valued was established, it became automatic. We get great at the things we practice and I had practiced this behavior so long that not only was it comfortable, it was all I knew. It was good enough. So was my relationship with Clark. I was staying the course.

If that meant getting a job, I would get a job. Once I learned that working part-time would be sufficient, I embraced the idea.

After attending a course in Chicago, I became certified as a Pilates instructor and started teaching at the Y. Then I spent some time learning how to teach indoor cycling and after working for a few months got to know some of the athletes in town. A few of the women who took my cycling class invited me to join them on outdoor rides and I took them up on it. As my fitness improved, those rides kept getting longer and longer. They started out as two-hour rides and then went to four-hour rides and eventually even six-hour rides were common.

The thing about riding with people for extended periods is that you get to know them really well. Something about the rhythm of pedaling must loosen the tongue because after a while the normal social barriers come down and you learn "the rest of the story." I was on a sixty-mile ride with three women, all ironman triathletes, when one of those eye-opening conversations began.

"I have to change my anti-depressant cocktail because I'm just not feeling very good these days," said Jen in passing.

"I switched from Prozac to Zoloft and I feel way better," replied Anna.

"You guys are kidding me!" I interjected. "You're the happiest people I know. I can't believe with all the triathlons you do plus how fit you are that you actually take anti-depressants!"

That was a mistake on my part because they thought I was judging them. Honestly, I wasn't. I was just shocked.

"Oh, I don't take much…just a half a pill works for me," said Anna. "Sometimes I feel really low otherwise. It keeps me happy."

Jen, on the other hand, was clearly insulted. She didn't mince words. "Look, I've struggled all of my life with depression. It's been horrible at times and I've tried everything. Not everyone has a perfect little life like you do."

We were heading into the wind, slightly uphill and I was feeling strong so I gradually picked up the pace.

"I don't have a perfect little life," I said. "I've had my share of problems."

And before I could say anything else Jen, trying to hang on to the faster pace, started yelling at me.

"Yeah, right. You can eat whatever you want, you barely work, and you have the perfect family. You have no idea what it means to struggle."

And then it happened. Out of nowhere, I just spit it out.

"Yeah Jen, it's been a fairytale, all right," I yelled, sarcastically. "Including the time I was raped. Yeah, that was a blast. I was fifteen, he knocked me out and I came to in the middle of it...boy was that fun!"

I picked up the pace again, leaving them behind. Up until that moment, I hadn't allowed the world to know. I wasn't looking for sympathy and I didn't want the memory of the assault in my head. But more than that, I still didn't want to be *that* girl. I liked the image they had of me: the fun girl with the perfect life who ran around motivating people...now I was going to be judged. Now they'd think of me as the girl who was raped. God, I wished I could take it back. I eased back on the pace and waited for them to catch up.

Rhea was the first to speak.

"Wendy, I'm sorry," she said. "I never would have guessed. Look, I've had bad things too. My dad was in jail for a while when I was growing up and I hated being that kid. I think we've all got something."

"Ok, so I read you wrong. But you hide it well," Jen offered sympathetically.

And then Anna opened up with the divorce of her parents and their subsequent absenteeism in her life. We spent the next two hours of the ride talking about our respective struggles. It was quite the bonding experience and Rhea was right: all of us face challenges in life from time to time. It's part of the human condition.

I felt like we were in some kind of club after that ride. Each of us had shared stories that we'd never shared before and I realized that each of our adversity experiences, although very different, resulted in a similar outcome. All of us worried too much about what everyone else thought. As a result, we were surviving our lives more than we were living them. We looked successful on the outside but when it came to the way we were getting through life, not one of us was driving. Jen was probably the closest. She was at least in the driver's seat with her hands on the wheel, steering. Rhea and I were more like front seat passengers, making suggestions about the direction we should take. And then there was Anna. Anna was in the backseat staying out of trouble, just going along for the ride. We were quite a foursome but our friendship deepened after that discussion and we became a support system for each other.

Not long after that ride it occurred to me that my friendship with them and the other cyclists/triathletes in our training group was having a positive impact on me. I even joined the local triathlon club so I could spend more time with them. I was regaining a level of fitness that I hadn't had in a very long time and along with it came some well needed self-worth. It was amazing to me how much my friendships were impacting me, even as an adult.

As parents we often worry about the quality of our children's friends. We know that "hanging" with the wrong group might lead to unnecessary trouble for our kids. But we don't think about our own friendships in the same way. We should and need to! When talking about the quality of someone's diet I used to say to my friends, "You are what you eat." There is some truth to that statement but I think I like the phrase "You are who you hang out with" even more. No matter how old we get or how much living we've done, we're still influenced by the people with whom we spend the majority of our time.

When my kids were babies, I hung out with the other stay-at-home moms in my neighborhood. We supported each other with kid issues and dinner issues and yard issues and sometimes even husband issues. We were a great resource for each other and at the time I thought we'd be close friends forever. We even promised each other we'd never move, at least not until we moved into assisted living together. However, as our children grew up and we moved in other directions, our friendships changed.

Think about that for a minute. As we travel through life, we also tend to travel through friends. Although the best connections will last a lifetime, some are meant to be transitional. Let's say, for example, that your life has changed and you value health and fitness more than you used to but spend most of your time around people who still eat out all the time, watch a lot of TV and drink a lot. If that's the case, your health and fitness goals probably get pushed aside more often than you care to admit.

That doesn't mean you have to abandon your friends completely, however. That would be like throwing away those favorite shoes that secretly hurt your feet. You wouldn't do that…you love those shoes. However, they're impossible to wear for long periods of time. You might show up to a wedding in them but when it's time to dance, they come off. You wear a pair of comfortable shoes that are better for your feet most of the time and bring out those favorite shoes for special occasions. Likewise, with your friends, you would be wise to spend the majority of your time with people who "fit" your life, with people who are a reflection of the kind of life you want to live.

The unstated assumption here is that you have a clear vision of the kind of life you want to live. That requires self-esteem. Without it, the kind of life you think you want to live is likely to be the kind of life the people who influence you the most want you to live. With self-esteem, you have vision about who you are and what you value so you can choose the influences that best support that vision.

My new YMCA friends had a strong focus on health and fitness, which I also cared about so they were great for me. Katie, a triathlete from my Pilates class, even downloaded the book, "The 7 Habits of Highly Effective People," by Stephen Covey onto my iPod. This was a book that'd been around for a long time but it was new to me and perfect timing. I'd head out to the trails at High Cliff State Park and run, listening to Covey's prescription for living a proactive life…things like, "The most important ingredient we put into any relationship is not what we say or do, but what we are." I loved it. I even took time to develop a personal mission statement because it made no sense as he put it, "to work really hard, climbing the ladder of success, only to find out it's leaning against the wrong wall."

So there I was, hanging with people who gave me confidence while listening to a book that encouraged my ever increasing self-esteem. Consequently I changed the way I thought about my life. I started to look at it as a gift and knew it was my responsibility to take great care of that gift. I was finding control and as a result, I stopped acquiescing so much at home.

If Clark liked anything, it was predictability. I had been the peacemaker for our entire marriage and peacemakers don't rock the boat. I was rocking the boat and it was frustrating for him. Mind you, I never had any premeditated plan to frustrate my husband. I just started to stand up for myself more often, even when it made him unhappy. Instead of dwelling on it, I focused more on my kids, my new friends and my fitness. I also competed in my first triathlon and did so well that I raced in three more. The sport of triathlon was quickly turning into a way of life for me. It marked the beginning of a process of change that would continue for the next 5 years.

CHAPTER 6

"Are you saying you're happy to be unhappy because you've been unhappier before?"
RHEA KRATZER

If you think you can't, you can't

That September, after Gina had settled into her college routine and the boys were back in school, I went to Madison to cheer for my Ironman friends and got caught up in the excitement of the race. At 7:00AM the race started and I watched as 2500 people swam the 2.4 miles in Monona Lake. Next, I drove around the 112 mile bike course looking for my friends and cheering like a crazy person. Finally, I rode my mountain bike back and forth over the 26.2 mile run course trying to offer encouragement to the extremely tired legs of those who could still run. It was over at midnight and I was exhausted from spectating. However, the joy in the faces of the finishers was compelling and I decided it was a challenge I wanted to experience.

The day after an Ironman event is the only registration opportunity for the following year and I found myself sitting at the computer waiting for a chance to lay down $450.00. I fumbled through the online process but got it done. I was registered for Ironman Wisconsin 2006. I bought a book that was supposed to guide me through the process and started training. I also started going to a masters swim class and began weight training. If I was going to do it, I was going to do it well.

When an Ironman event is off in the distance, it doesn't weigh you down much and the training is fun. However, as the date approaches look out! You start to worry, especially when you've never done one before. By mid-summer, I was consumed with second thoughts. Plus I was struggling with a foot issue. On top of that, the deadline for withdrawing from the race and still receiving a partial refund was fast approaching. The stress of competing in an event of this magnitude was overwhelming so I decided to let my first half-ironman race speak for me. If it went well, I would stay the course and if it didn't, I'd hit the refund button.

It didn't. The Racine Half Ironman was a qualifying event for Nationals. It's known to be a fast course and people throughout the Midwest showed up for the event. It was my longest effort to date so I didn't know what to expect. In the end, the swim went as planned, my bike split was commendable, but the run was torture. It was hot, 85 degrees, my legs felt flat, and my foot issue was debilitating. The farther I ran, the more it hurt and I finished feeling defeated. I was fourth in my age group, twenty minutes behind the winner and I resolved not to compete in Ironman Wisconsin in September. I wasn't ready and I knew it. But more than that, I was afraid of letting people down. In my mind, everyone expected me to do well. Winning at shorter distance triathlons was one thing. Translating that success to the Ironman distance was another thing all together.

Sometimes the patterns we establish in life are so ingrained that we have a hard time breaking them, even when we know better. At this point, I was well aware of my tendency to worry about the judgment of others. I knew better. But I still worried and convinced myself that racing would be a disaster.

As soon as I got home from the Racine race, I signed onto my computer, pulled up the Ironman website and hit the refund button. Immediately I was relieved. I called Rhea, my closest friend, and shared the news.

The previous year was Rhea's first Ironman. This year she was competing again and on schedule to improve significantly. We did most of our training together so she was dumbfounded.

"You're kidding me! You did great at Racine! Wendy, you've done all the training. I can't believe you really bailed," she said.

"I couldn't, Rhe," I replied. "My Morton's neuroma is too severe. I just can't imagine trying to make it through a marathon."

"I know but it's still seven weeks out. We'll find a solution for the foot thing and besides you'd be so fast on the bike that you could walk the whole marathon if you wanted."

No, I didn't want to do that. If I was going to do the event I was going to do it well. I couldn't bear the thought of people watching me and judging me for walking. Then it occurred to me that I wasn't even listening to Rhea. She was trying to give me support while I was trying to justify a decision I made that really had little to do with competing. It was about the fear of failure. The problem was I had already failed. I failed because I quit. At that moment I wanted to be more like my older brother. He would never have quit...any outcome would be better than quitting.

Doug was extremely confident. He was 6'5", athletic, and easy on the eyes but that's not to say he didn't make mistakes. He made more than his fair share. He was a social kid who made the most of his popularity. There was the drinking and pot use in high school that turned into more serious drug use in college. My brother was a musician. He was a voice major in college who made a hobby of the electric guitar. Doug was a huge fan of Jimmy Hendrix and was proficient at his version of the National Anthem. Honestly, he sounded just like the record. He was on the ten-year plan in college because of the detours he took along the way, but he graduated, funding the final years of his education on his own. After college he continued to pursue his passion for music, playing in a few bands but eventually he started a magazine. His magazine, The Metropolitan, struggled for several years, but Doug believed in it and today it's a great success. He's still a musician too, however now he sings Frank Sinatra in night clubs for fun.

Doug faced plenty of challenges along the way but he kept moving forward and he never quit believing in the things he loved. He didn't care what anyone thought of his mistakes, either. He owned them all because he understood, just like Dad taught us, that the challenges he faced would make him stronger in the long run. Doug had vision. He was driving his way through life. I guess all of those years he spent bouncing around off-road paid off. I needed some driving lessons. It was time to worry less about what everyone else thought. I knew that but didn't know how to get there.

For the most part, I was relieved to have the stress of Ironman off my back. It was easy to swim, bike and run with my friends just for the fun of it. But then I received a letter inviting me to Nationals. The top five finishers in each age group at the Racine race received an invitation to compete and that included me.

The National Championships took place in St Louis, just a week after Ironman Wisconsin. St Louis was eight hours away, far enough that I could have a second chance at the half distance without anyone around to see how it turned out. The idea was appealing because it gave me a chance to save face plus expectations wouldn't be very high. So I hired a coach, Jim Boldra, a twenty year veteran of the sport, to better prepare myself for the event and spent the next six weeks getting ready.

When September came, I headed to Madison to cheer for my friends once again. I had mixed feelings about missing out on the race until the weather made me grateful to be on the sidelines. It was cold and rainy and it stayed cold and rainy all day. Even spectating was miserable. Many people struggled out on the course, however, my friend Rhea had a great day, finishing and hour and a half faster than the previous year and she was excited to travel with me to St Louis the following week. But first, I took the time to register once again for Ironman Wisconsin. I wanted another chance. There was something about the discipline, focus, and challenge involved in getting to the starting line of an Ironman that scared me, not unlike my life scared me. I wanted to conquer it.

Rhea and I drove straight through to St. Louis the following Thursday, debating whether or not we needed to stop for gas. The two of us had some great adventures together over the past few years and since neither of us had any sense of direction, we were always surprised when we found our destination without some major detour. We laughed about those trips including the occasional times we managed to get lost in spite of having a GPS along telling us what to do. We also spent hours talking about fitness on that drive, trying to solve the problems of the world.

"Have you ever noticed how so many of the people who work out at the Y seem to be trying to lose somewhere between ten and twenty pounds and they come in month after month and year after year but hardly anybody ever changes?" Rhea asked.

"Whatever made you think of that?"

"Well, I don't know," she replied. "I guess sometimes I feel like one of those people."

My friend Rhea just finished an Ironman. She is one of the fittest people I know but she's not a tiny girl. She's strong. Compared to the general population, she looks incredible. However, she hangs out with elite ultra-distance athletes and consequently she feels too heavy. So I had to give her some perspective.

"Rhe! Have you lost your mind? You're amazing!" I said. "Think about Joanne."

Joanne is a friend of ours and a personal training client of mine who's a hundred pounds overweight. She's desperate to lose weight but often overwhelmed by her compulsions. Her patterns around food are so ingrained that even when she plans ahead it's hard for her to stay on course. She'll manage for a few days but then something will happen that derails her effort. She's been to the Duke Fat Camp, she's hired nutritionists, she's worked with psychologists and of course she has tried most diets. She struggles with self-esteem plus some of the people in her life aren't very supportive so the road she is traveling is particularly difficult. I've been working with her for over a year and even though her fitness has improved, she hasn't lost much weight. I'm humbled by her struggle.

"Oh, I know," said Rhea. "Joanne's in good company too. Maybe in some ways the guy at the Y who's trying to lose ten pounds isn't so different from her. He's not getting there either."

"Wow, Rhe, I never thought about that. He probably goes home and does some of the same things that Joanne does. Most of us have some habits around food that aren't healthy," I said. "For example, if you have a habit of eating in front of the television and you substitute carrots for potato chips, you still have the habit of eating in front of the television. I think people have to change the habit. They either have to give up the snacking or give up the TV."

Rhea didn't laugh. "I hate the way you talk about weight. You always make it sound so simple. It's really annoying. There's nothing simple about it," she said.

"But I'm serious. Think about it," I said. "Once the pattern is established, every time you sit in front of a television, your mind starts begging for food...even if you're not hungry. It has to be torture."

"Well, that's true," said Rhea. "That's why I spend so much time sewing. I can't eat and sew at the same time. I only get into trouble with food when I'm bored or tired."

"That's what I'm talking about. You don't have any food associations with sewing, but you have plenty of them with boredom. And even though you're aware of it, you still find yourself in the kitchen randomly rummaging through the cupboards, right?"

"Yeah, well you're pissing me off. It's way more complicated than that. Trust me, I know. There are plenty of really famous people out there with unlimited resources who can't figure this problem out so I'm pretty sure you're not going to solve it either. Besides if everyone suddenly ate less it would be bad for the economy," Rhea said. "The goal of the food industry is to find ways to get us to eat more."

I laughed. "And that's reinforced every single time we go to a restaurant. I always eat too much when I eat out."

"Yeah and last year I actually gained weight while training for Ironman. I was training 20 hours a week but I was so tired that I was eating more thinking it would give me energy. I should've just sewed all of the time."

"Well maybe that could work for you, but most people don't sew," I added. "We should come up with a list of all the things you can't do and eat at the same time."

So we worked on the list for a while. Then I added, "I'm sorry the weight thing is hard for you. I don't mean to make light of it. I spent too many years judging myself by how I looked in a mirror, Rhe. I hope you know how amazing you are."

"Thanks but in the future don't compare me to Joanne. It doesn't make me feel better."

"I was just trying to give you some perspective."

"Really?" she asked. "That's like saying someone else's lousy marriage should make you feel happy in your own. Does it?"

"Well, maybe, kind of. Whenever I think about how awful my marriage was with Dick, it reminds me that this one isn't so bad."

"Hello, you're not making any sense," said Rhea. "Are you saying you're happy to be unhappy because you've been unhappier before? You're always telling people to be great. Well, I don't think there's anything great about that."

"Wow," I replied, trying to process what she just said.

After a few minutes of uncomfortable silence Rhea continued, "Look, I've got this tire around my middle and I hate it. Everyone always tells me I look fine. Do you want it?"

"No," I answered.

"So don't try to make me feel better about it. If you want to support me, push me toward my goals. Tell me I can get there, unless you don't think I can."

"No, I totally think you can. I know you can," I offered with conviction. "But Rhe, you said something more important than that. When we compare a situation we're dealing with to something worse, we just end up lowering the bar. Thinking about the ways things could be worse might make me feel better about my situation but you're right, it doesn't make me happy. That kind of thinking just stops us from dreaming, from moving forward. You just made me realize that I do that."

"Well, how 'bout we promise to always push each other to be the best possible version of ourselves, how 'bout that?" she asked.

"Deal," I said.

Rhea and I could talk about anything. Periodically we'd get annoyed with each other but in the end we always worked it out. We spent so much time training together that we knew our friendship was bigger than any issue. She was the perfect travel partner for this trip because she completely distracted me from the challenge ahead.

The race course in St Louis was hilly, especially the run, and I was nervous the days leading up to it. I promised Jim I'd hold back on the bike and save more energy for the run; my foot issue had been resolved thanks to cutting some holes in the insoles of both shoes. However, I didn't go into Nationals with a lot of confidence. I was still afraid of the distance. The memory of the Racine event was fresh in my mind and there were many talented athletes running around looking impressive.

In a triathlon, athletes are expected to prepare for the unexpected by carrying supplies with them. For example, it would be foolish to race without carrying a spare tire and air cartridges. Even though there are support vehicles on the course, it's the athlete's responsibility to fix a flat and get back into the race. On race morning I chose not to attach my repair kit to my bike. Without it a flat would end my day. It would provide an excuse, a reason not to run, a way to save face if things weren't going well. I felt extremely anxious all morning, making several trips to the bathroom. Still, I knew I was better prepared for this race than any to date and as I headed down to the water, Rhea reminded me to trust my training.

In the end, I had a great swim. The fifty-six mile bike segment was going so well that by forty miles I was talking to my tires, begging them to stay inflated. The last thing I wanted was a flat. Transitioning from the bike to the run, I still felt great and held it together to the finish line. Rhea was cheering for me down the final stretch, yelling all kinds of "I told you so" statements in my direction while she jumped up and down. It was an extremely satisfying day.

Hiring a coach and going into the race with a game plan paid off. My time was fifteen minutes faster than Racine on a much more difficult course. I even won my age group which gave me a spot on Team USA and an opportunity to compete in the ITU (International Triathlon Union) World Championships in Australia in November.

Earning a spot on Team USA was one thing. Finding a way to pay for a trip to Australia was another.

CHAPTER 7

"The most important races are within and the love we share with others is the prize we take home with us" PAUL KORDUS

Driving Lessons

The World Championships were just 8 weeks away. I couldn't afford to go and I wasn't about to ask my husband. No, we already had that discussion the month before. It didn't go well.

"Wendy, you're spending too much money on this sport. You need to stay on a budget. I expect you to make enough to cover all of your triathlon expenses from now on," he said. "Think about it: you spent $40.00 on Powerbars alone last month and I'm not taking money out of the family budget to pay for your coach."

There was something about the tone of his voice that cut through me. Clark spoke in absolutes, no room for discussion. I didn't bother to respond. He had made himself perfectly clear.

I took a part time job at the new running store in town and I started teaching Pilates at Lawrence University. But those jobs weren't going to cover a trip abroad, especially one coming up so soon. However, my friend Tim stepped in and started a fundraiser for the trip. Tim headed up the donor relations office at a university so he was comfortable asking people for money. He was also a great friend of mine and an avid cyclist. We had spent many hours training together that summer along with an eclectic group of competent riders. These people had a lot to do with my fitness on the bike but even more to do with support and friendship in my life. Once the fundraiser became a reality, Clark softened. He said I could go if it didn't cost him anything. Sometimes he made me feel like a child who needed to get permission from a parent. Thankfully, my brother along with Peak Performance Physical Therapy, many cycling friends, and some other close friends contributed so the trip was on.

Less than two months after Nationals I was on a plane to Canberra, Australia. For the first leg of the trip I was by myself but by the time I was getting on the main flight in Los Angeles, I was meeting fellow Team USA members. It was a trip I'll never forget because it challenged me in so many ways. It was my first time traveling without friends which felt lonelier than I expected. Plus the distance of the race was closer to an ironman than a half-ironman, the swim was actually longer. Then there was jet lag to contend with, which was more challenging than I anticipated. For the first several days in Australia I was tired and my legs didn't cooperate on training rides. I didn't feel normal until the day before the race. And finally, I had a young roommate who stayed out late most nights. She was involved in a bike crash two weeks earlier so she couldn't run. She had come for a different kind of fun.

On the plus side, the Team USA organization took great care of us. We had a mechanic on hand who was extremely competent plus a team doctor, a massage therapist, and two coaches. They had activities planned for us along with the events associated with an ITU World event, like the nations parade and opening ceremonies. The activities helped but overall my confidence was on a rollercoaster ride. Fortunately Jim anticipated my emotions. When I called he continually reminded me that I'd do great if I believed I'd do great.

"You've done the work. You're ready for the distance. You're going to feel great on race morning. Just trust yourself and don't worry about anyone. Take in the day and celebrate everything it gives you."

I listened. He was helpful, as were the friends who sent e-mails. I tried to lean on them leading into the race, even though they were 9000 miles away. I needed their support because I was spending too much time second-guessing my decision to participate in such a big event. In a way, the trip was turning into a driving lesson. I couldn't stay in the passenger seat in Australia. There were over two hundred athletes on my team and a handful of people to help us. We were expected to be self-sufficient.

On race day I was on my own. 5:00 AM on Sunday morning in Australia was 2:00 AM on Saturday morning in Wisconsin. I thought about calling home before I left the hotel but decided not to. I was as ready as I was going to be. It was a mile walk to the race venue, a silent procession in the dark as everyone was focused on the day ahead. The feelings I went through that morning made me realize how much I appreciated my support group back home. It was a reality check because even though I was becoming more confident, I missed that security blanket of friends. Heading into the water that morning, surrounded by hundreds of athletes, I felt uncomfortably alone.

In the end, I swam and biked well. No surprise there. But the 18.6 mile run was tougher. I was passed in the first of three laps by two women in my age group. I passed one of them back in the second lap and caught the other one in the final mile. She looked spent so I passed her but she saw the age printed on my calf and passed me back. I didn't care. I was pretty sure we weren't in medal contention and the day had gone better than expected. With just a half mile to go, it was all about holding it together. As I crossed the line and the announcer broadcast my name and third place finish, I was stunned. That was incredible to me and just eight seconds out of second place! But I didn't see anyone in the crowd that I knew. I had no supporters. It quickly turned into the strangest "alone" feeling I had ever experienced.

What good is success if the people who matter in your life aren't there to celebrate with you? Accomplishment for the joy of accomplishment is another variation of doing the right thing just because it's the right thing to do. It requires centeredness. I didn't quite have that yet so I was looking for an external source for validation, searching the crowd for a familiar face. The sadness I felt and the internal struggle I experienced in those first few minutes after the race overwhelmed me with emotion and I started to cry. However, I realized what I was doing. Then I remembered my coach's words, "Take in the day and celebrate everything it gives you." The day gave me a lot. I tried to calm down.

The second place finisher, and elfish woman from Australia, found me minutes later and greeted me with a huge hug, thanking me for the extra push. That gesture turned me around. She felt like surrogate family. We headed to the lake to chill our legs and were quickly joined by athletes from all over the world. We huddled there, in cold water feeling for each other as we replayed the day. That was my favorite moment of the trip, all of us standing there in waist-deep water: different countries, different languages, different experiences, but somehow the same. The next day I walked into town, sat on the steps of an office building and watched the patterns of the people milling around, lives moving in different directions, dealing with any number of challenges. It was fascinating to me that I would never know how any of their stories turned out. Those people were like books I hadn't read and would never have the chance to read. However, I was the author of mine and while sitting there, I decided my story should have a happy ending. Later that afternoon I joined my teammates for the awards banquet and closing ceremonies. The next day I was heading home with a bronze medal, just in time for Thanksgiving.

Thanksgiving is a holiday that I have never shared with Clark. He's a deer hunter as are most of his siblings, so his family tradition is to hunt from dawn until dusk every day during that week. He has Thanksgiving with his family in Merrill while the kids and I have Thanksgiving at home with my family. This year was no different, but after a week of sitting in the woods and thinking about life, Clark wanted to talk more about the money situation. When something was weighing on Clark's mind and he was ready to talk about it, he would schedule the conversation, not unlike you'd schedule a meeting at work. I knew going into the discussion that I wasn't going to argue. I just wanted to borrow some time.

"Hon, I know Ironman is a big deal for you this year but you need to keep your spending in line," he said, matter-of-factly. "This year I expect you to cover all of your expenses, including the miscellaneous stuff like eating out or going to happy hour with your friends on Fridays. You're making enough money to do that and it would take some stress out of my life."

"How about this," I said. "I'll do my best to cover my expenses and if you support me with all the training I have to do this year, I will get a full-time job after Ironman and give it all up. How's that sound?"

Oh, he liked the sound of that all right. I was well aware that Clark wanted me to get a "real" job. He had to work full time so I should have to work full time. He thought it was only fair. He wasn't worried about after school time with the boys nor did he care about cooking and cleaning. Money was more important or was it control? I was having too much fun while he toiled away at work. He didn't want me to be unhappy but he wanted my life to parallel his. The world according to Clark was becoming increasingly structured and it was frustrating trying to fit into the box he built for me. He wasn't interested in my dreams. He was blinded by his vision of what he expected from our life together. Fortunately, I had an entire year to think about his vision, a final year to fulfill an Ironman dream.

I had such a great experience in Australia that I kept my coach during what I knew would be my last year of triathlon training. With thirty Ironman events under his belt, Jim added the perspective and experience that I needed to succeed. I trusted him and followed his training program to the letter. I biked exactly how far and how fast he wanted; I ran with a heart rate monitor to stay within his prescribed training zones; I did the swim workouts with his list of drills; and I even stretched, rested and fueled according to his plan.

Rhea was on board with Jim too. Her training was going great and although she didn't have an Ironman on her schedule, she earned a spot on Team USA for the 2007 World Championships in Lorient, France in July. I wasn't planning to go to France until Rhea got in. Suddenly we had the chance to go together and oddly enough Clark didn't seem to mind. When I asked to stay for a few extra days to do some recreational cycling with Rhea, he even suggested we stay for a week. So we did. It was the most unstructured week of our lives. We knew we were going to spend the extra time in the Loire Valley biking and visiting castles but that was the extent of our planning. We had no reservations, no schedule, and spoke very little French. A friend lent us the guide book, *France for Dummies*, which ended up being a constant resource. With the book in hand it was easy to find lodging and easier to find great food. When we got lost, we just pretended we wanted to go wherever we ended up. The trip felt like a vacation from life.

My arrival home was a reality check. It turned out that Clark had decided to remodel the kitchen "for me." He took a week of vacation and managed to do most of the work himself and he was pretty far along when I returned. I was stunned. I was also confused. He spent $25,000 on a new kitchen without even mentioning it. Wow! What happened to the budget? I thought about the loans we took out for Gina's education. I thought about the conversations we had regarding my spending habits. And now we were adding a second mortgage for a new kitchen? The whole thing seemed incredible to me. He picked out the tile and the cabinets and the countertops. He laid out the design too. He made all the decisions and told everyone that he was doing it for me. I knew I was supposed to be grateful but come on, $25,000 without any input from your spouse? It was going to take a while for me sort that out.

In the meantime, it was done so I decided to go with the flow. There was still painting to do and that was my department. After the kitchen investment, I decided he had no right to nickel and dime me over everything I bought. It wasn't like I was the kind of wife who went shopping for the fun of it. I was tired of the parent/child approach he used with me when it came to money. If he could spend $25,000 without talking to me, I could buy new basketball shoes for Matt without getting permission…and I did.

Between training for Ironman, finishing the kitchen, and chasing after the kids, the balance of the summer was a blur. I was grateful to have Gina home from college. She had a full time summer job but didn't go into work until 1:00PM. She was happy to watch her brothers' in the morning which freed me up to train and I used that time to train with greater focus than ever before.

I learned over the course of the year that the discipline of fitness was as good for me as the fitness itself. Though I did not always want to get out of bed for the early morning workouts, especially if it meant swimming, I did. The satisfaction I felt afterwards impacted the way I viewed myself. As the race approached, the hours invested in training continued to increase. During the final ten weeks, I was working out twenty-plus hours a week. The commitment was huge but the benefits were worth it. I started competing in this sport because I liked hanging out with my "Iron" friends, but in the end I was doing it for me and it felt great. As September approached I was confident about this Ironman and couldn't wait for the day to arrive.

CHAPTER 8

It's supposed to be hard; if it wasn't hard everyone would do it. Hard is what makes it great. – TOM HANKS

Ironman

It was race morning, 4:30 AM, and I was up partly because I didn't really sleep and partly because it was time to eat breakfast. I was staying at a fellow athlete's home in Madison with my coach, his wife, and four other friends. We called it the Iron Inn and the parents, who were retired, spoiled those of us who were lucky enough to stay with them. I was trying to eat two pieces of toast with peanut butter plus a Powerbar before we headed over to the race. I was feeling extremely emotional that morning so I wasn't the best company but everyone understood. They'd all been in my shoes before. My expectations were high and my training had gone very well. Most people thought I could break thirteen hours, but I secretly believed

I could finish closer to twelve and a half hours. My coach believed it, too.

We pulled in to the venue around 5:00 AM and I headed to body marking, the spot where volunteers write your race number on one of your arms and one of your legs with a permanent black marker. Then it was over to my bike which I had checked in the day before. I added my fuel to the bike and pumped up the tires while my friends dropped off my special needs bags. Then it was rest time, focus and visualize time, listen to music time, try to relax time. I'd been training for Ironman for two years and the day had arrived. At 50 years old, I was the fittest I had been in my entire life and more confident. I was excited to race, but relax? Hardly. However, there was nothing to do for the next hour so I decided to lie down by my teammates. I closed my eyes and thought about my dad.

He died earlier that year around Easter, April 4th to be exact. He had a stroke and we had Hospice care for him at home for his final nine days. We didn't have a funeral. My dad was about celebrating life, not crying about death. Besides, he never really left. He'd been with me throughout the entire Ironman journey. Sometimes while riding my bike into a headwind, it would feel too easy. I'd laugh at the thought of my dad gently pushing my bike to help me along. I talked to him on a regular basis as did my mom but her pain was different. The hole he left in her life was deeper than mine. Maybe the magnitude of your love is directly related to the depth of that hole. Maybe the overwhelming sadness she felt was a testament to the greatness of their love. I felt oddly jealous that my mother had 53 years in a relationship that was so precious to her. She was lucky. It'd been six months since his death and Mom was still teary at the drop of a hat. Gina had been right to worry. Even with family by her side, Grandma felt alone. She had to go to bed every night without Dad and none of us could make that easier for her.

I could, however, remember the example that he set and celebrate the life I was living. I had every intention of doing that today. Whatever happened, good or bad, didn't really matter. What mattered was that I enjoyed every second of the day. I was going to take it all in and celebrate everything it gave me.

A teammate nudged me. It was time to head down to the water. Finally! Oh, one more trip to the bathroom! The sun was just coming up and while walking to the beach, I was in line with a sea of black wetsuits. I got in the water and swam out to my predetermined starting spot. My coach planned everything for the day, including the spot where I seeded myself for the start. So there I was, treading water with 2500 of my new best friends and I was crying. I wasn't the only one either. Many sacrifices are made on the road to becoming an Ironman. Every athlete in the water with me had a story, every athlete faced challenges along the way. The journey is personal and sometimes emotional. My tears were a combination of nerves, anticipation, and a realization that this could be a once in a lifetime experience. I was in the water. I was really going to do an Ironman...today! I cried some more.

"Oh great! Come on, girl," I thought, "Get it together!"

I was crying so much that I had to take off my goggles to dry my eyes. Then, I was struggling to get them back on, hoping the gun didn't go off before I was ready.

"Ok, come on, settle down a little," I thought nervously.

I was having quite the conversation in my head. Then they played the National Anthem and my tears started all over again.

"Crap," I thought, "this is a disaster before it even starts."

Fortunately that thought made me laugh and then BANG! We were off.

Just try to imagine 2500 upright athletes going horizontal in that instant. Mayhem! Bodies on top of bodies, people were under me, over me, kicking me, pushing me...it was incredible! I was laughing and swimming at the same time, trying not to drink too much water as the commotion made it impossible to fall into a rhythm. It took almost a half mile before the swimmers started spreading out and then finally I found a nice pair of feet to draft behind and settled in. Swimming is noticeably faster if you can get in the draft of other swimmers. It was another skill that I learned and practiced many times thanks to my coach. I was feeling great. I was also well aware that the swim would be the easiest part of the day, so I tried to enjoy the next two miles.

An hour and fifteen minutes later, I was out of the water a full five minutes ahead of schedule. I felt insanely happy as I plopped myself in front of the wetsuit strippers so they could pull mine off. Then it was a run up the helix, past a boisterous cheering crowd. I knew exactly where my friends would be standing so I was looking for them. When they started cheering the tears came back to my eyes. Oh yeah, it was going to be a day to remember!

Ironman events are impressive for many reasons, but the number of volunteers on hand to support the athletes is mindboggling. Over 4000 people donate time to pull off this event and some of my favorite ones are the volunteers in the transition area. They'll do anything to help you short of changing your clothes for you. They'll pull your stuff out of the bag, put sunscreen on you, and even clip your helmet. All I had to do was grab my cycling shoes and head out to the bike corral.

I loved my bike. It was new, a gift from Tony Free at Griffen Bikes. Ironman was my first race with the new bike so I couldn't get on the road soon enough. Biking had always been my strength but I had to be careful. I knew if I went too fast on the bike, I would pay for it on the run. Jim explained this to me ad nauseam.

"In an Ironman," he'd say, "it's not who's the fastest, it's who slows down the least."

I listened and wasn't about to blow it. Feeling better than ever and paying attention to my legs, I stayed light on the pedals but still, my average speed was 19mph and that was too fast. When I saw my coach halfway through the bike course, he was already reminding me about the run. Yup, I was going too fast, but honestly, it felt like I was floating. My legs were telling me that 300 miles, not just 112, would be fine, so I held on to that pace. However, lactic acid started to build in my legs during the last ten miles back to the transition area and that worried me.

When I returned to transition, a volunteer took my bike and I ran inside the building to drop off my helmet and jump into my running shoes. I was about a half hour ahead of schedule at that point and had no idea how much longer the euphoria would last. I expected things to get tougher but was determined to follow my plan as long as possible. The next goal was to manage the marathon by running for four and a half minutes and then walking for thirty seconds over and over again until I crossed the finish line. The run course was out and back two times so it was easy to break it down into four separate runs of six and a half miles each. That was exactly what I did.

The first run went well. I ran into my kids about six miles in. Chad wanted to jump into my arms but I had to discourage him. I was pretty sure we both would've hit the pavement. I stuck to the plan and actually gained some time during the first leg. The second run, which got me to the half-way point, went nearly as well. I held on to my pace and was still well ahead of the original goal. Next came the third leg and the struggle began. I could tell that my body was ready to call it a day but I hung on. I was excited to see anyone familiar because encouragement means everything when you find yourself in uncharted territory.

Then reality set in and I suddenly admired everyone who had ever completed an Ironman. With six and a half miles to go, the excitement of the day was replaced with an odd combination of fear and determination. My stomach was bugging me, my muscles were screaming at me, and I had to coax my legs to keep moving. However, I was coached for that exact problem and knew what to do. Jim taught me to distract myself by visualizing success. He believed that the final miles of an Ironman are 80% mental and only 20% physical.

He'd say, "You're trained to go the distance. If you believe you'll make it, you'll make it."

Knowing what to do and executing it are two entirely different things. Sure, I was trained to go the distance and I believed in my training but mentally I was struggling. I had to find a way to believe in myself. People around me were already walking. I knew I could walk to the finish and still have a respectable time but I also knew deep down that I didn't want to give up on the plan so it was time to distract myself.

I focused on all the challenges I faced to get to that point. All of the 5:30 AM swims, all of the 100 mile bike rides, all of the pool runs during an injury, all of the ice baths to reduce inflammation after long runs…I thought about all of those things and reminded myself that the day was a celebration of those efforts. I forced myself to keep running. Then I thought about all of the friends who played some kind of role in my training and I knew they were celebrating with me so again I told myself that I had to keep running, just a little farther.

I stopped to use a port-a-potty hoping it would help my stomach problems. It didn't and I was so drenched in sweat that it was hard to get my shorts back on. Once back on the road, I switched over to thinking about my dad and I imagined what he might say.

'That's the old pepper, Woops!" he'd cheer with pride in his eyes.

God I used to love it when I was a kid and he'd say that. My childhood flew through my mind and settled for a short time on the rape. It occurred to me that it was never about me. In life we're limited by what we don't know, what we haven't yet learned. We're also limited by the things we believe but aren't really true. So the child in the Middle East who's raised to hate Americans grows up to be the man who gladly sacrifices his life to kill us. And likewise, the African-American child who is raised around prejudice and double standards grows up without any regard for my life. The late 60s, early 70s were racially charged years in my town. When I drove the boat to his side of the lake, I was someplace I didn't belong and he chose to take advantage of it. I couldn't forgive the choice but I could forgive him. So with each step, I let it go. Running was so painful at this point that there was real symbolism in the idea. I literally felt like I was letting it go. I realized for the first time that I wasn't *that* girl anymore. I WAS NOT THAT GIRL! My life was important and living it with focus suddenly mattered. That idea gave me strength and with more determination, I told myself to keep running.

    Finally, I was down to the last two miles and my friends were popping up everywhere. My coach showed up on his bike and started coaxing me to hang on.

"Wendy, if you can just hold it together, you will break 12 hours," he said with parent-like pride. "Come on girl, you've got a chance to do something great here."

He was excited and so was everyone else. My friends were excited because they were pretty sure I was winning my age group. They were excited because that would mean a trip to the Ironman World Championships in Hawaii. They were excited because it was my first Ironman and I was doing better than anyone expected. With a mile to go it seemed like everyone was screaming at me to keep running. I remembered my experience in Australia. I didn't want to see someone come by me with a big "50" printed on her calf. I dug deeper. My coach was close by again, willing me up the final hill, reminding me to hurry.

"Come on," he yelled. "You're almost there. Nice quick feet. You've got it now. This is your day. I'm proud of you."

I was trying and I was full of tears again, not because of my coach or my friends and not because I was making it to the finish line. I was grateful for all of those things but I was full of tears because I was making it to the starting line. I was driving and I knew it. I had both hands on the wheel with the gas pedal to the floor and even though the engine was falling apart, I felt incredible. I had vision. I was in control of my life. As I rounded the final turn and looked at the finisher's chute ahead, I could hear the announcer: "From Appleton, Wisconsin, first timer, Wendy Heldt ...YOU ... ARE ... AN ... IRONMAN!!"

I crossed the tape.

Part 2:
Getting it right

CHAPTER 9

Faith is not something to grasp, it is a state to grow into. MAHATMA GANDHI

The spreadsheet

Two months later, the emotion of the experience still resonated with me. Nothing had changed on the surface. I had the same kids, same values, and same friends. But I was anything but the same girl. A light had turned on that wrapped me in warmth and love. I felt unusually introspective, trying to understand the bigger picture. The unique way events crossed my path and impacted my direction weighed on my mind. There was a spiritual quality about it but not one that sent me back to church.

I had been exposed to a variety of Christian faiths growing up, baptized Lutheran, confirmed Methodist, and as an adult, converted to Catholicism. I liked reading about religion, mine and others. I taught religious education for seven years but eventually concluded that when it comes to faith, the devil really is in the details. The more specific we get, the more divided we become. So I gave up on the details and accepted a broader view. I preferred the mystery. I was more comfortable with a less defined concept of God, convinced that the details didn't matter. What mattered was how we treated each other.

Post Ironman however, I wrestled with several ideas. The balance between ego, humility, sacrifice, and self-worth played in my head. Yes, we need to value each other but also ourselves. No one defines me; I define me. No one can limit me; I limit me. The quality of the life I live depends on me, on the value I assign to it. Or is it a gift to me because I'm connected to something bigger, something I can't define? We're all connected to something bigger…equally.

I kept sorting through these ideas, sometimes empowered by them, sometimes humbled by them, but more than anything feeling grateful for them. I felt like I had been asleep for thirty-five years, living a chameleon-like life, adapting to the demands around me. Now, suddenly, I was awake and excited about it. However, I put those thoughts on the back burner when my husband handed me a spreadsheet.

In one column there was a chronological list of my year to date expenses and in the other column a list of the money I had earned. At the bottom he deducted the income from the expenses and there was a total due of $2000.00. Then he told me he expected to be paid. Wow! The detail was impressive and the time he must have spent putting it together blew my mind, but the fact that he expected to be paid surprised me.

"Do you really want me to pay you back?" I asked.

"That's the deal we made last year. You said you'd cover your expenses and you didn't. You can't spend money you don't have."

"Right, and like you had the money for the kitchen?" I asked rhetorically.

"That's different. The kitchen was an investment. I'll get that money back," he said. "Talk to your friends. I bet they'll think you should pay me back."

"Seriously? You seriously think my friends will support you on this?"

I took him up on that challenge. In the days that followed I presented the spreadsheet to my friends who thought the situation fell somewhere between hilarious and dysfunctional. One of my girlfriends has a popular morning radio show. She threw the situation out to her listeners who were unanimously brutal to Clark. A week later I gave him a watered down version of the feedback but he held his ground. He couldn't understand how anyone could find fault in his thinking.

As I studied his efforts that first night, I actually felt of proud of myself. Imagine that, only $2000.00 in the hole and I had gone to France earlier in the year. Without that trip, I would have been way ahead of the game. And considering I had no idea the France thing was going to happen when I made the deal with Clark last November, I didn't feel bad about it.

The spreadsheet was a wakeup call. The more I looked at it, the more bizarre it seemed. I wasn't his wife anymore. I was a business partner and because of that, I decided to pay back every penny. It was time to get a real job. The reality of this decision had weighed on my mind for a long time. It was the other half of the deal I made with him and now, even though I was headed to Hawaii next October, making money needed to be a bigger priority. I had a plan for that but it would have to wait for a new day. It was late, the kids were in bed and I was exhausted. As I headed upstairs, Clark intercepted me.

"Hey, do we have a date tonight?" he asked.

What the hell! Was he out of his mind? In our house a date meant sex.

"I think I'd prefer to pay off my debts before going on any dates," I responded. "But thanks anyway."

He walked away. I was done. I definitely was *not* the peacemaker anymore. I remembered the line from that poem again: "I want to know if you can disappoint another to be true to yourself." Yes, I could. I went to bed.

✭ ✭ ✭

I had spent some time over the previous year thinking about what kind of career I could get excited about. I thought about all of my prior work experience and realized the job I loved the most involved writing and delivering training programs for a bank. I liked it because I had a lot of autonomy and because it was rewarding to travel to various locations and facilitate training that improved banker/customer interactions. I was an internal consultant to the branch presidents; designing programs that helped them reach their goals. Unfortunately, that bank had since merged with another bank and the role no longer existed. Fortunately, I had a more exciting option. I had a connection in the consulting industry.

I can't emphasize enough how important it is to make connections as you travel through life. Not only do they offer perspective, but connections open doors to new opportunities when you need them the most. Steve Kuper is the owner of Innovative Learning Strategies (ILS), a leadership consulting firm. He was a Pilates student of mine. We became friends over the years and have had a few conversations about working together. Steve specializes in the areas of leadership, executive coaching, culture change, and dysfunctional team interventions. I like him. Unlike many training companies that present programs that quickly get filed on a shelf, Steve facilitates change. He treats his clients as if he has a vested interest in their success. He is one of those rare people who always does the right thing just because it's the right thing to do. I respect him. I knew this would be a good match for me and finally the time was right. The time was right for Steve as well. He was busy and he was ready to take me on. This was great news because it gave me options and I needed options to have control of my direction.

Steve allowed me to jump right in. He gave me way too much rope and I hung myself a few times but he took it in stride. I credit him for having faith in me and I never wanted to let him down. He also gave me the flexibility to train for Ironman Hawaii and to get home most days at 3:30 for my boys. I was busier now than I had been in years and although my workouts were suffering, I loved the new direction. So did Clark. He loved it because more money was coming in. I loved it because it would eventually be my ticket to freedom and as the year progressed I felt confident enough to talk with him about a change of direction.

We sat down after the boys were in bed and I could feel the tension in the room. He sat across the room from me with a furrowed brow and pursed lips. His arms were crossed. He was obviously uncomfortable so I took control.

"I know you're not happy and neither am I," I confessed. "Truthfully, I'm not sure I can remember a time when I was really happy with us. When I look back at it, we've always struggled with each other."

He agreed. Clark was a man of few words and these conversations were particularly hard for him so I was being careful.

"I think we drove each other crazy even when we were dating," I continued. "But the timing was right and our relationship looked good on paper, right? I mean, we were both athletes and had many of the same friends and you wanted a family and I wanted more kids. But we never had a great connection. You're black and white about things, charts and graphs...so much so that sometimes I think your mind is a computer. And I'm all over the place. I act and then deal with the consequences the next day, right?"

"I agree with all of that," he said defensively. "I'm not happy with our situation but I don't think I should have to change either."

I was with him there. We had plenty of compromise discussions over the years and we were both tired of trying to meet in the middle.

"No," I said. "And neither do I. I think we're such polar opposites that trying to change hardly scratches the surface. I think you should be yourself in the world and you should be married to someone who loves you exactly as you are."

His eyes widened and he was looking confused so I decided to take the blame.

"Clark," I said. "When you married me, I was a mess. I wasn't particularly strong. I didn't stand up to you and was willing to just live in your world. But I've changed and now I'm really a pain in the ass. That's not your fault. You are who you've always been. If you're anything, it's consistent. I think you need someone who's a bit more predictable in the world and that's not me."

I could tell he was waiting for me to lower the boom, but I wasn't thinking that way.

"Look," I continued, "We both love the boys and we want to do what's right for them. Staying together would probably be good for them so I'm not opposed to the co-parenting idea. Besides, the financial nightmare of the divorce scenario would probably kill you."

He actually chuckled at that and I could see the relief in his eyes. I wasn't done yet. The conversation was going better than I had expected so I kept talking.

"I think we should just stay the course until the boys are grown, unless you meet someone. You're going to think this is a little weird but I have to tell you that I would love for you to have a satisfying relationship with someone who adores you. I know it's never going to be me so if you found that opportunity, I'd move and I wouldn't be mad."

He looked at me like I was from another planet. "Really."

"Yeah, really," I said, adding, "Clark, I don't think you are a bad guy; you're just not right for me. I want you to be happy. So let's just raise these kids together and if something changes we can talk about it."

He leaned back in his chair and relaxed.

That was the crux of it. We sat there for quite a while talking about the mess we made of things over the years and laughed about it. We both felt better after that conversation. He even thanked me for it. We weren't pretending anymore and we actually managed to get along a little better. I also realized how little emotional connection I had with him. And, I was honest about hoping he'd find someone someday. However, I didn't expect the same for me. I decided that I missed it and at this point in my life, I really didn't care. I cared about four things: My kids, my career, my friends and my fitness...and probably in that order. Above all else, I wasn't letting my life happen to me anymore; I was making it happen and for the most part, I was looking forward to it.

Looking back on that year, Ironman landed me firmly in the driver's seat of life but not because of my race day experience...race day was an exclamation point. The big changes happened en route and many of them were directly related to the company I kept. I learned that the relationships we foster in life, personal and professional, are a significant part of our success. But equally important is the ability to believe in ourselves. Instead of looking to external sources for validation, we should find it from within. We are precious. Our lives are priceless. I finally understood what self-esteem felt like. It was only after gaining a little self-esteem that I realized I'd survived so many years without it. If someone had suggested earlier in my life that I needed it, I would have laughed. I was always the girl who could walk into a room of strangers and quickly make friends. I was outgoing and gregarious so I thought I had plenty of self-esteem. But it's not a characteristic that's defined by personality style. It's defined by an internal love and appreciation of the gift of your own unique life. It grounds you from the inside out. It helps you become centered. People with self-esteem can give to the rest of the world without losing their sense of self. They're driven by their values and their vision.

In contrast, I spent most of my life trying to balance my values with the expectations of others. I was judging myself from the outside in as opposed to the inside out. I was blind to this pattern because I was so accustomed to it. Besides, I liked who I was. I just didn't think I deserved to live a great life. That sounded egotistical. I thought we should be more humble, grateful for what we had. However, true personal humility isn't possible without self-esteem. When we're driven by our values, ego and pride are softened. It's no longer about the spotlight; it's about an unyielding resolve to do the right thing. We *are* supposed to live great lives, with both passion and humility.

Just when you think you've got it figured out, the world throws more perspective at you.

CHAPTER 10

You can search throughout the entire universe for someone who is more deserving of your love and affection than you are yourself, and that person is not to be found anywhere. You yourself, as much as anybody in the entire universe deserve your love and affection. BUDDHA

Your *self*

I thought I had it all figured out after Clark and I settled into a co-parenting relationship, but I was wrong.

We stayed the course, neither of us wanting to create unnecessary drama in the lives of our boys who were just finishing fifth and third grade. We both wanted what was best for them but as always, our approaches to discipline were miles apart. Clark wanted lots of it and I wanted as little as possible, especially when it came to the small things. A good friend once told me that great parents say "yes" whenever they can and save the word "no" for the important stuff. I spent my time telling the boys how amazing they were and

Clark spent his telling them what to do. Of course, I'm exaggerating but that's how it felt. He was about rules. The fact that I didn't care about the details frustrated him. We were silently driving each other crazy. Summer couldn't come soon enough in 2008. I was acutely aware that I had another Ironman looming and Gina wasn't home to help with the boys. I was also traveling for Steve so keeping balance in my life was harder than it had ever been before. Something had to give and for me it ended up being television. I was not proud of my TV habit, which I blamed on all of the frustration I dealt with earlier in my marriage. When I turned the TV on, no one would bother me. I became one of those parents who yelled at her kids from the couch instead of getting up to see what they were arguing about. I remember it all too well; the boys would be downstairs fighting and I wanted them to stop.

"Knock it off down there!" I'd yell.

And if that didn't work, it sounded worse.

"Guys!" I'd yell louder. "If I have to get up and come down there, you're both going to your rooms!"

And finally, if that didn't work, it sounded worse still.

"Ok, that's it!" I'd holler, finally getting up and walking to the top of the steps. "Both of you, upstairs now! Hurry up!"

On his way up, Chad would try to reason with me.

"But Mom…"

"No buts! I don't want to hear it. Just get into your room!"

And up the stairs they went. They'd slam their doors too but I didn't care. I just wanted to watch my show. I returned to the couch.

It's embarrassing to think back on that. I had absolutely no idea what they were arguing about and really didn't care. How sad is that? I couldn't juggle all the balls in my life anymore if I kept watching TV. I needed to spend more time with the kids as well as force myself to get to bed earlier so I could get up and train before heading to work.

Giving up television was hard because I watched so much of it. I thought about it for weeks before taking the plunge but the rewards quickly made it worth the effort. I started playing more board games with the boys and was surprised at how quickly they lost interest in their gaming systems if mom wanted to play chess or better yet, Othello...the super easy strategy game that your third grader will quickly learn how to play and kick your ass. Trust me, it was humbling. If we weren't playing a game, we were shooting hoops in the backyard or playing our version of touch football. I had to admit, giving up TV made me feel great on the inside plus it put some balance back into my life. I was also sleeping more which gave me more energy, making it infinitely easier to get up when the alarm went off in the morning.

The summer of '08 flew by and as the boys started school again, Gina was entering her final year of college. She had one more semester at River Falls and then she was spending her last semester in Europe with the traveling classroom program, thanks to the generosity of Grandma and Uncle Gary. They wanted to "broaden her horizons" which really meant "get her away from the boyfriend." But Gina beat them to it, finally breaking up with him over the summer. We were all happy with that decision as Jay had no direction, bouncing from job to job, playing video games and partying with his buddies. I was proud of her for moving on although it was a difficult process because he was her first long-term relationship.

College was great for Gina. She spent two of her college years working as an RA and consequentially helped several students through some tough situations. As a result she was becoming quite an amazing young woman. I even listened to her advice from time to time.

"What's the matter Mom?" Gina asked. "You look grumpy."

"Nothing really, I just went to the store and Dad's pissed because I forgot a few things. He's mad because I didn't make a list."

"Why didn't you make a list?"

"I never make a list," I said. "I'm not a list person."

"Did it ever occur to you that you might not make a list because you know Dad wants you to make a list?" she asked. "Think about it Mom. What's so hard about a list?"

"I don't know. Does he have to get mad about it?"

"No, but Mom, I've heard you challenge Dad when he says 'no' to the boys over something really stupid," she said. "Not making a list is like saying 'no' to Dad over something really stupid. I think you should make a list."

I made a list.

As we moved through fall, I took my trip to Hawaii for the Ironman World Championships. It was an emotional trip for entirely different reasons than my first Ironman. This time I was saying goodbye to the sport. My priorities had shifted. There was no support at home and I was more focused on my career so I decided to let it go. Hawaii was a great place for that. My coach came along to support my efforts as did a girlfriend of mine who was in need of a vacation.

Ironman Hawaii was huge in every way. All of the big names in the sport were there along with tons of media and manufacturers of everything related to triathlon. It was incredible and my emotions were high leading up to race day. I had downloaded, "A Moment in Time" by Whitney Houston and every time I listened to it on my iPod, I started to cry. Still, I listened to it a lot, over and over again and so I cried a lot too. As my coach, poor Jim didn't know what to do with me when the tears fell.

However, on race morning I felt pretty good. The race venue was insane with media. I walked through a sea of telephoto lenses as I headed over to the bike coral. I checked my tires and memorized my spot before heading to the ocean.

Treading water, while waiting for the gun to go off in Kona, was less of an emotional experience because I knew what to expect plus the ocean was beautiful. For much of the swim, there was a colorful display of tropical fish entertaining me twenty feet below. The waves and the tide were challenging but I was a stronger swimmer than a year ago and felt at home in the water. It was by far my favorite part of the day. Coming out of the ocean I felt great but my training leading into the event wasn't as good as the prior year and I was quickly impacted by climate challenges. Fall training in Wisconsin did nothing to prepare me for the heat. The comfortable sixty-degree days I enjoyed leading up to the race were and night and day from the 108 degrees of heat coming off the lava rocks on the Hawaii course. The fun and excitement were gone about halfway through the bike section. I was getting dehydrated but didn't realize it because the wind evaporated my sweat, disguising the effects of the heat. By the time I made it to the run I wasn't feeling good and spent the marathon doing as much walking as running. The toughest part of the run course is closed to spectators. For about fifteen miles the athletes are alone, except for fueling stations. I had to depend on myself to find the motivation to finish.

Walking alone in the dark, I realized how much the Ironman experience mirrored my life experience. Just like life, the idea of competing is exciting but the reality is full of challenges and unexpected adversity. Just like life, the experience is unique for every person who's brave enough to show up at the starting line. And just like life, overcoming the most difficult obstacles, makes us stronger, better, happier. If it was easy, it would be forgettable. It's the challenge that makes it meaningful.

At the awards banquet the following day, I couldn't help feeling disappointed over some of the mistakes I made out on the course. The race was still replaying in my head as the announcer introduced Dick and Rick Hoyt, a father/son team who were about to be inducted into the Ironman Hall of Fame. Rick has cerebral palsy but thanks to supportive parents, he's lived a full life. Even though he's a quadriplegic with an extremely limited ability to speak, he went to public school, eventually earning a college degree. When he told his dad that he wanted to run in a charity event for an athlete that was paralyzed in an accident, Dick pushed his son in a wheelchair through the entire five miles, trying to run the distance for him. Later

Rick told his dad that during the race, he felt like his disability disappeared. That was the beginning. Thirty years later Team Hoyt has competed in nearly 1000 races including four visits to the Ironman World Championships. To succeed at Ironman Hawaii, Dick drags his son through the swim on a raft, then pedals up and down the mountains on a custom bike with Rick sitting up front, and finally he pushes him through the marathon in a three-wheeled chair. Dick provides the engine and Rick fuels it with his heart. During his speech, made possible through computer-voice technology, Rick said if he had a healthy body, the first thing he'd do is put his dad in the chair and push him. His message was about love. His message was about believing in yourself. His message was about what you *can* do. I didn't feel sorry for him. I was in awe of him.

The Hoyts reinforced in my heart the benefits of centeredness and perseverance. Even though my day didn't go exactly as planned, I finished and wouldn't trade a minute of the experience.

✪ ✪ ✪

Fall turned into winter and the holiday season. The year was topped off by a New Year's Eve party at the home our masters swim coach. Most of us were triathletes and we were in the mood to drink and celebrate another great year. I invited a friend that I wanted to introduce to the group. Hendrik was relatively new to the area, also a triathlete, younger than me by twelve years but tall, 6'6", and scary good looking. Running into this guy always made me happy and I knew everyone would like him. Instantly, he was a hit. Later in the evening, I was standing next to him, my back to him, slightly in front of him while talking to a girlfriend and he gently placed his right hand on my right hip. The effect that had on my body was incredible. You would have thought I was having sex or something. It was all I could do to remain calm. Of course, he had no idea and I wasn't about to say anything, but the inside of me was in overdrive.

A few days later I was relaying the experience to Katie over a few glasses of wine. I told her it felt like a wakeup call. It was as if he turned on some kind of switch inside me and I didn't want to turn it back off.

"I can't understand why I reacted like that. It should have been nothing but it was incredible. What if it's not just him? What if it happens again and I'm stuck in this compromised relationship with Clark?" I asked. "What then?" And I added, "All of the sudden everything feels like such a lie and I hate that."

Katie wanted to know why I was still living with him in the first place.

"Look," I explained. "I don't want to bounce the boys around. I don't have enough income to buy a home and I don't want to stress Clark out with the nightmare of a divorce." I added, "Plus, I'm the buffer. I make the kids feel good even when Clark is frustrated."

"The boys probably know more than you think they do," she suggested. "My parents didn't have a good marriage and we all knew it. They stayed together for us but I don't think it helped us. We grew up with role models that didn't like each other. I'm telling you it wasn't good."

"Yeah, well I really don't have any easy options right now."

"Maybe you should just live here with me and John for a while. We have plenty of space and you could come over after the kids go to bed."

John and Katie lived four blocks from our house and they were longtime friends of mine. I thought about that idea for a while and decided it had legs so I talked to Clark about it. I told him I wanted to live an honest life but I didn't want the boys to suffer and I didn't want him to have to move. I suggested that living with the Kellys might be the perfect solution. I could be home with the kids after school until bedtime and then I'd leave. No one's life would be disrupted and the kids could adjust to the idea of us loving them but not living together.

"Yeah that would work," he said with barely a blink. "Since I'm taking the boys skiing this weekend, why don't you just move your clothes over there while we're gone?"

Just like that, we were separated. The boys were initially upset with the news but it was soon forgotten because their lives really didn't change very much. Dad was in charge of the morning routine so that was an adjustment but otherwise things were pretty status quo. We even continued to have dinner as a family and within weeks Clark surprised me with a conversation about filing. Turns out he'd been thinking about the financial side of a divorce for quite some time and he was ready to head down that road. We used the same attorney and in the end we split our assets but I agreed to forgo child support and maintenance so long as the living arrangements continued to work out. Our divorce was finalized in just four months and although we've had some bumps along the way, it's gone better than either of us expected.

That's not to say we didn't struggle with the normal emotions connected to divorce. Oh no, it's never easy. Truthfully it's incredibly hard with so many unknowns. We made it look easy because we didn't fight and because we managed to put the kids' best interest first, but both of us suffered. Fortunately the economy took a dive and Steve's business slowed enough for me to take some time off to get it together. Both Clark and I lost weight and we were challenged with redefining ourselves in the world. We also had to deal with the rumor mill and work on establishing new ground rules for each other. Everything changed. When I was married, I was trying to hide from my husband, wanting to be left alone. Now I was divorced and painfully alone. I was ridiculously happy some of the time and unbearably sad other times. My emotions were all over the place but the storms I had weathered earlier in my life helped me realize that these feelings were OK. Plus I was driving this time so even though I felt out of control from time to time, even though I felt depressed from time to time, even though I felt lost from time to time, I knew it was temporary.

Whether I liked it or not the alone thing was an adjustment. There's an introspection benefit about it that's worth the sadness but not when it lingers into the next day. I also think there's an aspect to happiness is practiced. To some extent, if you act happy, you feel happier. The same can be said of sadness. I didn't want to spend much time practicing that behavior so I took advantage of some coping skills that helped me feel like myself again.

First there was my "spot." It's a place in the woods, on the back side of a state park about twenty minutes from my house. It's not new. I found it shortly after I returned to Wisconsin when Gina was just a baby. My parents' home was adjacent to the park and shortly after we moved in with them I discovered the trails. While running one day, I took a detour that brought me to a clearing. After jumping a small ravine, I found myself standing on the edge of a cliff so I sat down and looked out at the lake. The view was great. No people, just me and Mother Nature. The wind would blow through the trees like it was trying to have a conversation with me and I loved it. During those first few years back in Wisconsin, I developed a relationship with that spot and have never stopped going there. Sometimes a year or more would pass without a visit, but when the course of my life started to change, I returned more frequently. I'd show up with the sadness of the entire world on my shoulders, but as I'd sit and listen to the wind, those feelings would dissolve. Whenever I was in the woods, I felt connected to something bigger and would always leave feeling better. So during the transition from unhappily married to divorced, I often headed out to my spot.

Another thing I did more than ever before was read. I was having a hard time one day and a friend suggested I read "The Alchemist" by Paulo Coelho. Now there's a book that speaks to you when you are trying to take charge of your destiny. After reading that, I followed it with everything else Coelho wrote. Sometimes sitting down with a great book would have an effect on me similar to hanging out with great people. It would inspire me and give me perspective.

Listening to music was another outlet that helped. I developed a more personal relationship with music during that time in my life. Even though I grew up during the rock and roll explosion, I wasn't a kid who had a stereo in her room. I wasn't out buying records or eight-tracks or cassettes or CDs. However, when I received an iPod for Christmas four years ago, I quickly made friends with iTunes. A song was just ninety-nine cents and soon I was making playlists. There was a playlist for running, another one for driving the car and, after moving out of Clark's house, even one for when I felt sad. On the worst days it felt like my soul was bleeding. So I'd get my iPod and pull up my sad playlist. I'd lie on my bed, listen to it and just wallow in misery for a while. I wasn't really crying; it was more like my eyes sprung a leak and the tears just poured out. After about an hour the music would transition to lighter, more upbeat songs and that change in tone would help me feel like myself again. I know it sounds a little crazy but I always felt so much better afterwards. It was sort of a meditation experience for me. You could do the same kind of thing in a yoga class…well, except for the tears.

My iPod, my spot and reading became my favorite "alone time" activities. I've learned that it's important to like the company you keep when no one is around. But there is one other thing I've always done for my soul: I love exercise. Sure it's good for your body but it's much more than that for me. I've had the discipline for such a long time that it's just what I do. For me, it's as important as brushing my teeth, especially when I'm sad. I sometimes had to push myself out the door but EVERY time it made me feel better.

I always end my Pilates classes with the same tagline: "Take care of yourself, because you're worth it."

If you're going to sit in the driver's seat and make your life happen, you'd be wise to take care of the vehicle. Your body is a gift and the only thing that no one can take away from you. It goes wherever you go. The way you look is the first impression you give the world. So when it comes to who you are, the cover of the book should represent the content.

"Take care of yourself, because you're worth it."

I said that for so many years without hearing the words. "Take care of your *self*," the inside of you, your soul, that which connects you to God or the universe. You can't take care of your 'self' until you decide you're worth it. Once you make that decision, you start to become more centered and you can decide what you value the most. Only then will you find vision for your life and begin doing the right things just because they're the right things to do. When that happens, you're driving.

CHAPTER 11

A mother is the truest friend we have, when trials heavy and sudden, fall upon us; when adversity takes the place of prosperity; when friends who rejoice with us in our sunshine desert us; when trouble thickens around us, still will she cling to us, and endeavor by her kind precepts and counsels to dissipate the clouds of darkness, and cause peace to return to our hearts. ~WASHINGTON IRVING

Yacht Worthy

Even during the saddest of times, I never questioned the decision to get divorced. After it was over, I felt like a bird that had been let out of a cage. I wanted to fly.

I was at Gina's commencement in May of '09 and the speaker, who was struggling with an illness, told the graduates to live their lives with as few regrets as possible. He told them not to worry about getting a job, but to find a passion instead and to always keep in mind the things in life that really matter. He closed with this James Dean quote: "Dream as if you will live forever, but live as if you will die tomorrow."

It was as if he was speaking to me. I hugged him afterward, embarrassing my daughter to no end. Later in the afternoon, Gina and I went book shopping to kill time before her graduation party. We couldn't find a bookstore in River Falls so we ended up at Shopko. After wandering around the store for a while, we decided to park ourselves on a couch we came across in the furniture section.

"You were lucky to have such a great speaker, you know," I said.

"Mom," she replied. "The whole time he was talking, I was thinking about you and how much you probably liked it."

"I know," I said, "I needed it but so did you. This is another beginning for you. You're going to face lots of changes and that's not easy."

"So how are you doing Mom? Do you ever see that tall hot guy?"

"Hendrik?" I asked, laughing. "So funny. Actually, he's a pretty good friend of mine but he's more like a brother."

"Sure Mom, that's why you're blushing."

"I'm not blushing!" I said. "Look, Hendrik is just passing through and I know it. He's in between relationships and wants to stay that way. Besides, the guy dates thirty-year-old women."

"Yeah, but you're still attracted to him. I can tell."

"Sure I am," I confessed. "Most of the time I feel like a school girl when I'm anywhere near him. There's an aura about him that's incredibly seductive. I think he affects everyone like that but it's not the way he looks that draws me in the most Gina, it's the way he acts. He's kind, polite, respectful, driven and soulful, on top of all of that hotness! He's a 'do the right thing' kind of guy. Truthfully, he reminds me of your grandpa but trust me, he's also careful not to give me the wrong impression."

"That is so sad."

"No, not really. It sounds sad because you're twenty-two," I said, smiling. "It's more like a gift to me. I'm just finding balance in my life and I'm excited about it. Hendrik gets it. He tells me I'm becoming more of me. I think it's the nicest thing anyone ever said to me. I love the thought...becoming more of me. I will say though that I wish I had waited to meet someone like him when I was your age."

I should have expected her next question.

"So why didn't you?"

"Great question, Bean. Why do so many marriages fail? People are making the biggest decision of their entire lives, arguably the decision that impacts their happiness more than any other, and they end up playing Russian roulette because they weigh the wrong things." I continued, "Everyone wants to be loved.

So when someone falls in love with you, it feels good and if he is a nice person, you get involved in his life. Think about your relationship with Jay. If you were a little older when you met him, what do you think would have happened?"

"I know," Gina replied. "There was a long time where I thought I might marry him. I kept waiting for him to get it together."

"But Gina, think about how he made you feel," I said.

"Oh yeah," she said. "He always put me down. He said I couldn't have a conversation about anything important. He made me feel stupid because I didn't read the paper."

"Right," I added. "And who was in college getting mostly "A's"? It wasn't Jay. He was controlling, too. He would get mad at you if you didn't call him every night or if you went out with your friends, remember? And you still loved him! I was extremely worried about you."

She leaned into me then and I put my arm around her.

"Sorry Mom," she said. "I was so caught up in him and how much he needed me that I couldn't see it. I'm lucky I was going away last summer. It gave me an excuse to get out. I'm lucky I have Ethan now."

I sat up taller and turned her face toward me.

"Gina! Ethan is lucky he has you. You are spectacular."

"I know Mom but he's really good for me," she countered, smiling. "Ethan is so easy. He's happy. He's optimistic. He believes in me and treats me like I'm precious."

"I know, honey," I said, "and if you marry him some day, I won't worry about you. I like him a lot. Just keep in mind that these are the years to keep both eyes open. If men were boats, Jay would have been a row boat. Ethan is, at the very least, a motor boat. No one wants a row boat when they can have a motor boat, right? And a motor boat is great until you see a yacht for the first time. And the yacht I'm talking about has nothing to do with money, Gina, it's all about character. Just make sure Ethan is a yacht, OK? You are definitely yacht worthy."

"Yeah and when Grandma saw a yacht for the first time she knew it, right?" she asked.

"Exactly," I replied. "But then Grandma expected to marry a yacht all along. She was so confident at your age that she was almost arrogant. Do you know the story of how they met?"

"In a bar, right?"

"Yup. Grandma was just twenty years old. She was at the Casino in Waupaca with a bunch of girlfriends when she spotted Grandpa sitting at the bar. She walked up to him and said, 'So are you going to buy me a drink or are you just going to sit there?'"

Gina started laughing.

"Grandpa said, 'What'll you have?' and Grandma's answer was, 'I'll have a ginger ale.'"

Gina laughed harder.

"Then she talked Grandpa into coming over and sitting at the table with her friends. Grandpa was thirty-one at the time and quite experienced with women. He'd never met anyone like your grandmother. Maybe that's the key. Maybe you have to know who you are first. Then you might stand a chance at marrying a yacht."

"Didn't you know who you were when you got married the first time?" she asked.

"Are you kidding me? I suppose I thought I knew who I was but in reality I was so caught up in pleasing the rest of the world that it's a wonder I didn't marry a raft."

Gina laughed again. "Well, you kind of did," she noted, adding, "But Mom, I still think you're yacht worthy."

"Aw, thanks babe," I said, kissing her on the cheek. "Come on, if we don't get up, someone is going to come over here and kick us out of the store."

✡ ✡ ✡

The combination of that conversation and the commencement speech left me walking around with mountains of regret over opportunities lost. This feeling continued to plague me until mid-summer when I was relaying those concerns to my mother. We were driving to Waupaca to visit Aunt Mildred, my father's older sister who was living out her final days in a nursing home.

"Sometimes I feel like I've wasted my life making mistakes," I said.

"Are you planning to die tomorrow?" my mother asked.

"No, of course not, but it's too late for some things. I just wish I made different choices years ago."

"I think you sound like Mildred," she said. "That's why she's miserable. She's so focused on the things that went wrong that she can't even remember what went right anymore."

My dad's sister was a great example of how low self-esteem combined with negativity can ruin a life. Most of Mildred's adult years were spent in New Mexico and Arizona because her husband had health issues and a warm climate was better for him. I didn't see her often until seven years ago when she came to Wisconsin to be closer to family. She was eighty-seven at the time and had survived a bad fall but not without complications. Mildred had been abandoned in a nursing home in Albuquerque so we basically rescued her and became her caregivers.

She was unhappy. She didn't have many friends, her children didn't communicate with her and in her eyes the world was incredibly unfair. Over the course of the last seven years, we'd heard about everything that went wrong throughout her life and watched her deflate those around her with a careful dose of arrogant superiority. It was amazing to me. She was my Dad's sister and they couldn't have been more opposite. Mildred was selfish and judgmental. She coveted what others had and was blind to her own gifts.

"What made her so negative in the first place?" I asked.

"I'm not sure," my mom responded. "Mildred wasn't a pretty child. She was tall and awkward and I believe her mother found her to be disagreeable. Instead of helping Mildred, she focused her love and affection on your dad."

"That wasn't fair."

"No, it wasn't. I don't have the whole story, but when your dad and I were first married, his parents and Mildred still lived in town. Her relationship with them was strained then so I'm fairly certain it had been like that most of her life."

"Guess I should be glad you like me, huh?" I asked.

My mom laughed and added, "It's really a shame that Mildred didn't get more support because she had some great qualities. She was a talented musician with the rare gift of perfect pitch and she was very intelligent. However, she never liked me. She thought your dad was too good for me."

"Yeah, Mom, that's obvious. When I visit Mildred on my own, she makes cutting remarks about you. But then she makes them about most people. She can really be mean."

"Yes she can," said my mom. "But underneath her bitter exterior, she's tender and incredibly sad. Mildred never fostered great friendships and consequently she's limited by a lack of support. She knows things will get worse, so they will."

"Ok, I don't want to be like that," I said. "It's just that I wish I had figured out my life sooner. Mom, I've been divorced three times. I've completely blown the love thing. It's a pretty hard thing not to regret. I missed that entire part of life. I'm 52 and I can't go back."

"I understand how you feel," my mom offered. "I've thought about that in regards to you too but regret is a dangerous thing."

Then an even bigger regret slipped out. "I wish I had never gotten out of that boat in the first place."

"Woops," my mom said, "you've come a long way these last few years but you're still missing a piece of the puzzle. You need to forgive yourself."

"What do you mean, forgive myself? I'm not mad at me."

If I ever questioned the wisdom of my mother, the conversation that followed put it to rest. She started with a question:

"What does the word 'forgive' mean to you?"

I should mention here that my mother's last name should be "Webster." When we were kids, we played word games in the car whenever we traveled. One of our favorites was making words out of the letters on license plates. We could make any word we wanted as long as we didn't change the order of the letters. For example, TNL could be "tunnel" but when it was my mother's turn it would likely be something like "international." Or BTN could be "button" but my mother would come up with "combination." Mom ruled.

"I don't know," I replied. "To stop blaming someone for something and make peace with them?"

"That's not bad. But if you look it up in the dictionary, it really means to give up resentment of or to stop feeling resentment against someone or something. Resenting someone takes energy and carrying it around is a burden. It makes you a victim."

"Yeah, Mom, I get that. And I forgave my rape. I had to let it go. Hating him just gave me a place to throw blame. It was like my problems were his fault so I always had an excuse. I know what you're saying, but I don't resent myself."

"Did you hear what you just said?" she asked, almost annoyed. "You said, 'my' rape. Wendy, it's not 'your' rape. It's his. It was his choice, not yours. It happened to you and affected you but it isn't something that you should take ownership of. It wasn't your fault."

She was right. I did make it mine. I never thought about it that way before.

"Yeah, ok, you're right about all of that," I agreed. "But I did get out of the boat. I wish I didn't do that. Hell, I wish I didn't drive the boat up to that dock in the first place. I had a bad feeling about it. My body had a sixth sense fear thing going on like crazy only as a fifteen year old I didn't understand it. I wish I could have protected the girl that I was."

"Yes, I do too. So that's what you need to forgive. Forgive yourself for getting out of the boat. And then forgive yourself for everything else you regret. All of that regret is a burden too. It's time to let it go. You've always tried hard to do the right things in life. I'm amazed at how willing you are to take the blame for the things that go wrong. From my point of view, they haven't been your fault." She continued, "It's time to put yesterday behind you. Listen, I've had a few big regrets in my life too and one of them pertains to you."

I thought she was going back to that toilet bowl incident but that wasn't it at all. She regretted missing my college graduation.

"Mom," I said. "I was fine with that. Your accountant was in from New York and the farm was in trouble back then. I understood."

Of course I was lying. My college graduation was a nightmare. Everyone I knew was surrounded by mountains of family, even distant relatives. I was graduating with the highest honors possible, alone. The contrast was too much for me. I understood my parent's dilemma but I wasn't fine with it; I was teary all day and couldn't wait to get out of my cap and gown.

However, sitting in the car, I could feel my mother's regret and added, "You had no choice."

"No, we always have choices," she said, reaching over and taking my hand into hers. "I made the wrong one."

Then we decided to forgive ourselves for our mistakes and promised each other that we would move forward in life living every day as if it might be our last.

I learned from my mother that forgiving myself was as important as forgiving anyone else. We've all made mistakes and in the process created some of the problems in our lives. If we could hit re-wind maybe we'd change a few things. But we can't. All we can do is learn from those mistakes and build a brighter future for ourselves. It's unfortunate that I spent so many years surviving my life instead of thriving in it. But I had to let that go in order to get excited about the future.

CHAPTER 12

Twenty years from now you will be more disappointed by the things you didn't do. So turn at once to your willing crew and sail away from the safe harbor. Catch the trade winds in your sails. Explore. Dream. Discover. – MARK TWAIN

Traveling

After that, each day mattered a little more. I began thinking about the things I've always wanted to do and just started doing them. First, I went to Eugene, Oregon to compete in a marathon. After the race, I did some sightseeing and got lost among the trees on Spencer's Butte. I spent hours in the woods, not knowing where the path was and not caring either. The view from the top of the butte was spectacular but the view among all the trees in the middle of the woods was more inspiring. It felt like my spot at the state park back home but on a much grander scale. Trees don't judge. They just exist so when you sit among them, you simply exist as well. The longer I sat there, the happier I felt. After a while, I laid on my back in a bed of ferns looking up toward the sky. The entire forest was hugging me and I could have stayed there for days. Pretty soon I was laughing. I was laughing for absolutely no reason and when I finally left, I wanted to cry.

In July, I spent a week on my bike in Iowa with 10,000 to 20,000 other riders as part of RAGBRAI (The Register's Annual Great Bicycle Ride Across Iowa). People come from all over the country for this 450-mile carnival experience. It's easy to eat too much pie because every church group in every little town offers multiple varieties of the best pie you've ever tasted. The towns lucky enough to host the cyclists each night are transformed into a "G" version of Woodstock. I had a great time but more significantly, made a friend that I will keep forever. It's not often that you meet someone and instantly feel like kindred spirits. Those relationships are special and although Jack lives in Connecticut, the friendship is easy. He's often the voice of reason in an unreasonable world.

I followed that with a trip to British Columbia in September for four days of sea kayaking with the whales off of Vancouver Island. I went to get away from the gossip in town. I wanted some time to assess my life and chart a course for upcoming years. Maybe this could have been accomplished at home but traveling was more exciting and nature always managed to give me perspective. I signed up with an adventure company. There were eight of us: three from Canada, two from Australia, one from Japan, one from New Zealand and me...plus two young guides who were also from New Zealand. I didn't go on the trip to be social but spending time with this diverse group made me realize that it's our uniqueness that allows us to add value. We are comfortable with people because of our similarities but we are interesting because of our differences.

The scenery was phenomenal. The weather was cool and often rainy but that was perfect for my mood. We spent four days on the water and camped on three different islands. For most of the trip, I felt like I was standing outside of myself, looking in and I didn't always like the view. I was replaying movies of my choices over the past year in particular, trying to look at myself more objectively. On the last day, I was sitting on a boulder in the middle of a rocky beach, looking at the millions of stones around me. As the waves came in, over and over again, they kept shifting the stones. It was mesmerizing and after a while it occurred to me that we are like those stones. When life shifts us, we land by new stones and learn new lessons. If we dig into the sand far enough, we can probably avoid the effects of the waves and keep things the same. I decided I'd rather shift and take in the next adventure.

I wasn't under anyone's thumb anymore. Each of those experiences gave me a broader perspective. I owned my life.

Later that year, I spent five days in Carson City, NV catching up with friends and attending the memorial service of a dear friend of mine who lost his life to colon cancer. Matt Ahnen was my age. I met him at a volleyball tournament in 1991. He was looking for his wife and approached me by accident. She and I could have been sisters we looked so much alike. From that chance meeting a friendship grew that healed the wounds of abuse from my second marriage. Matt and Lyn were givers. They worked hard, played hard and wrapped their friends in unconditional love. They surrounded themselves with like-minded people so a trip to their home in the suburbs of Chicago for a weekend of volleyball felt like a week-long vacation at a fancy resort. This group of people restored my faith in everything that was good in the world. I knew I'd miss them when they moved to Nevada 10 years ago and was crushed to learn of Matt's death.

Matt lived his life without regret. He was centered and all of us are better for having known him.

While there, I took a day trip to Lake Tahoe with some people I met at the service. We were having lunch when Sam confessed that he was unhappy with his marriage and thinking of leaving his wife after twenty-five years together. He wanted my advice. It's interesting to me how often I get this question now that I am "successfully" divorced. I asked him several questions to get a better feel for his situation and then offered some words of caution.

"I think you should be very careful about jumping ship," I warned. "Twenty-five years is a long time and probably worth fighting for. My situation is a little different because I never married for the right reasons in the first place. There was no foundation. You were in love with each other in the beginning. You had a lot of great years. It sounds like you respect each other and still communicate pretty well. Honestly, I have a feeling you're just bored."

"We don't do anything together anymore," he explained. "She has her friends and I have mine. We never have sex. I feel like there's nothing there."

"Look, Sam," I said. "My litmus test is this question, 'If you knew you would never find anyone again to build a life with, would you still want to leave your marriage?' I want you to really think about that. In other words, if it was this relationship or no relationship, what would you choose?"

"Oh, I'd meet someone," he responded, confidently. "That wouldn't be a problem for me."

"No!" I said. "You're not listening. I didn't ask if you could find someone. I'm asking you if your choice was to stay with your wife or be alone forever, which would you choose?"

"Well, then I guess I'd stay," he conceded.

"Then I think you should work it out," I suggested. "Really Sam, my advice is talk to her about your feelings, listen to hers and don't be afraid to get help. Leaving is hard. It's not fun. It actually sucks. It would probably be the hardest thing you've ever done. I think working it out is better unless you can't be yourself around her…unless the relationship is damaging to your soul. If that was the case, you would have answered my question differently. You would have chosen to be alone."

"What if I don't want to work on it?" he asked. "What if it's too far gone?"

"I don't know," I said. "I guess you and your wife are the only two who know the answer to that but I hope you talk about it over and over again before giving up. If you work it out, maybe when you're seventy you'll look back at the struggle with some fondness. I have a feeling it could be worth the effort."

I could tell from his expression that he was a little disappointed with the conversation. But I wasn't about to encourage him to leave. It's one thing to give someone advice, it's another thing altogether to assume you know what's best for them. That was his road to travel.

Fall turned into winter and I finished out the year with a trip to Maryland to visit my older brother. It was my first time back since his wedding twenty years ago.

When I got there Doug and Carol were in the middle of working on their top ten list.

"What are you guys doing?" I asked.

"Oh, it's just a New Year's tradition we started the year we got married. We can work on it later," my brother responded.

"No, don't do that. I'm interested."

"Ok," said Carol, "But first let me pour you some wine. A top ten list is best written under the influence of a little wine."

My brother laughed. Turns out, every year they sit down on New Year's Eve and try to pick ten things from the prior year that they hope to remember forever. They pick both good and bad things, accomplishments and regrets, milestones and fun little personal things between just the two of them. Now that they have twenty years of top ten lists, they enjoy looking back at the old ones as much as making the new ones.

Two glasses of wine into the process, while listening to them argue about whether or not the squirrel Doug had been feeding on the deck by hand should make the list, I was feeling unusually fond of them and commented, "This is the greatest thing ever. I wish Mom and Dad had one of these. Wouldn't it be cool to read the fifty-three years of their lives together? God you guys, I'm totally jealous."

Carol, smiling at me while picking out a new bottle of wine, said, "Thank you. You're so sweet. We look forward to the process every year."

Carol is a lovely girl, proper, almost formal because of her private school upbringing. I often wondered why she loved my brother so much because he was anything but proper. However, on this visit I learned that they've both mellowed, meeting perfectly somewhere in the middle.

While visiting them I connected with old friends including the man I dated in college. The years had been kind to him. Marshall was surprisingly the same happy, gregarious, confident guy I knew thirty years ago. We spent an evening laughing about the old days, all the while conscious of the energy between us.

When Marshall reached across the seat of his SUV, grabbed the back of my neck, and pulled me in for a kiss, it consumed me. When he wrapped his arms around me so I wouldn't go back into my brother's house, I melted into him. There was no space between us, physical or emotional. I hoped I'd see him again.

I did. Two months later, after a series of conversations, we connected again. This time we talked about the assault and the subsequent patterns I'd established over the years. We talked about my fears, along with the dreams we once shared and the life we've yet to live. And we enjoyed a lot of honest, passionate, uninhibited sex. I was wrong to think that men can't really tell what's happening to women sexually. I was wrong to think they don't care. Clearly some men care very much. The more I travel, the more I want to travel because it offers so much perspective. I recognize that regardless of socio-economic or cultural differences, we are more alike than different. We care about our families, our friends, our health and our planet. We want to live lives that matter, that make a difference. It seems simple but it's not. The thing that binds us more than any other is the complicated nature of the journey. We need each other. We need to communicate.

CHAPTER 13

"Nothing is impossible; the word itself says 'I'm possible'!" — AUDREY HEPBURN

Communication

My dad was right when he told my mom, back on the farm, that the difficulty they were facing would ultimately make them better people. It did. We learn this lesson over and over again because adversity is part of the fabric of life. Happiness comes from handling those challenges better every time, from doing the right things even when it's hard.

When we were kids, my dad spent countless hours in the driveway teaching my brothers and me how to play basketball. One of the first things he taught us was to look ahead.

"Come on," he'd say. "Keep dribbling until you know what you're doing with the ball."

In basketball you're dribbling, passing, or shooting. If you stop dribbling and pick up the ball without a plan, you're asking for trouble. Immediately, the other team will try to trap you and steal the ball. You have to look ahead to stay in control of the game. This rule is particularly important if you're the point guard because the point guard is the player who brings the ball up the court, runs the offense, sets up the plays and looks for opportunities to score. Even though my brothers and I were destined to be post players because we were giants among our friends, my dad still had us practice our dribbling skills on a regular basis.

Life is a lot like basketball in that you have to keep control of the ball if you want to score. We should be the point guards in our lives. God might own the franchise but he's not going to play the game for us. It's our responsibility to bring the ball up the court and set up the plays that define our success. We also need the right teammates. We can go a lot farther in the game if we recruit great talent.

When I look back on my life, I realize that after the rape, I lost the ball. As soon as I needed someone to approve of me, in order for me to feel good about myself, I wasn't in control of my life anymore. I wasn't the point guard...someone else was. All I was doing was running up and down the court. Sometimes I was sitting on the bench.

In basketball, when things aren't going well, the coach calls a timeout. He gives the players a pep talk and a plan to focus on. Most of the time, when they get back out on the court, they play better. Our closest friends and family are our coaches in life when we are struggling. They give us perspective and help us get back into the game. We're not supposed to go it alone in the world. We might want to sometimes but it's next to impossible to be objective with ourselves. All of us need the insight we get from others.

Fortunately, we are designed to connect. We want to be hugged and valued and loved. But we don't always want to be judged. It's the fear of judgment that keeps us from getting the help we need. We worry that no one will understand, so why bother?

Three generations ago, our lives revolved around extended families. If you didn't want to talk to your parents, grandma was waiting in the wings with the best stories. She could fix anything. These days, however, we're lucky to have family within driving distance, so our friends have to pick up the slack. Here's the big news...they want to! We just have to give them the chance.

So communicate and then communicate some more. Besides, saying what you're thinking is different from thinking what you're thinking. When you say it, you hear it. Sometimes just talking about something makes it better. Plus, every once in a while you'll say something, like I did on that bike ride years ago, and it will open the door for people to share things with you that they've been holding inside too long. As a result we become even more aware, understanding, connected, and ultimately happier.

My life might have been different if I understood that when I was fifteen.

Like all parents I have dreams for my kids. I want them to be happy and joyful. I want them to have passion for the direction of their lives mixed with compassion for the lives of others. And of course, I want them to be centered. So I've passed down those three rules I grew up with and repeat them every night as part of our bedtime routine.

The bedtime routine is my favorite part of the day, even on the ugly days when there's bickering, testing boundaries, and ignoring rules. I love the bedtime routine. It's quality one-on-one time. It's an opportunity to review the day and talk about challenges as well as accomplishments. It's a chance to affirm our kids and remind them how precious they are to us. It's even better than the quality time we get to spend with them in the car because the bedtime routine is an everyday thing. It's a tradition. If we recognize the great opportunity it provides us to bond with our kids, it becomes a chance to increase our relationship with them. Because of that, I'm careful about how I approach the end of my children's day.

I want to accomplish a few things every time: I want them to feel good about themselves, to know how precious they are, to understand that mistakes are OK, and to feel like they are in charge of their future. This is not the time for a lecture. Bedtime has to be a "feel good" thing. My children look forward to it because they trust that it's a safe, forgiving, and comforting time. It's not wise to try to solve the world's problems at bedtime. It's better just to put them to rest for the night with a positive thought.

We always talk about the day first. Sometimes the conversation is short and sweet because there doesn't seem to be anything pressing on their minds. Other times they unload their day:

"Hey Chad, anything great happen today?"

Lying on his pillow with his arms crossed he said, "No. I was totally bored all day."

"Really? Well, that's too bad. Didn't you have any fun playing with Alex?"

"Nope."

"Hmmm. Did you do anything that might get you in trouble?"

He put both hands on his face, hiding his eyes and then peeking through his fingers and grinning he said, "I threw Matt's basketball into the neighbor's yard."

"You did? Does he know about that?"

Back to arms crossed, he said, "Nope."

"Sounds like he made you pretty mad."

"Mom, when Alex and I came inside and went in the basement, all he wanted to do was play with Matt.

They were mean to me. Matt just took over. I hate him."

"Awe, baby, Alex is closer to Matt's age. That's going to happen sometimes. I guess I'd be mad too. You can be really, really mad at Matt but how about you don't hate him. He loves you."

"No he doesn't. He hates me too."

Brushing the bangs from his forehead with my fingers, I said, "He killed all the spiders in the clubhouse for you. That sounds like love to me."

Softening a little, he said, "Yeah."

"Do you think maybe I should retrieve the basketball for you?"

"Would you?"

"Sure. Listen, Chad, I'm sorry for ignoring you earlier when I was on the computer? You shouldn't have to ask me the same question three times to get an answer. Forgive me?"

"Actually Mom, it was five times but its ok. You're just a mom."

"Ha! You're such a smart boy and I'm proud to be your mom. Remember: treat everyone with respect, even your brother, do your best, and do the right thing just because…"

"It's the right thing to do."

"Good night baby, sweet dreams. I love you. May God bless you. Let the angels love on you."

That's usually the ending. The process starts the same with Matt but then it quickly transitions to a backrub. He lies there giving me instructions the whole time:

"A little to the right...now over to the left...now with just your finger nails...now circles....now with both hands..."

Sometimes I tickle him slightly, which always gets a response.

"Mom!" he complains.

When I'm done, I remind him of the three rules and then lean over and give him a kiss on the cheek.

"Love you so much," he whispers earnestly.

"Love you too Bud. Sweet dreams."

Matt is my emotional child. He wears his heart on his sleeve and feels his way through the world. The backrub puts everything to rest after a long day and I like watching him settle into it.

I did the same thing with Gina. No matter what kind of day they've had, I want my kids to go to bed feeling good about themselves. I know it makes a difference in their lives because of the quality of some of those conversations. Sometimes I think they save the important thoughts for bedtime. Like the time I was on my way out of Matt's room and he threw out a statement:

"I wish Grandpa was still alive."

I walked back over to his bed, sat down and got comfortable.

"Me too, what made you think of that?"

"I don't know. Basketball, I guess. Do you think he can see us? Do you think he can see me play?"

"Guess I don't know how to answer that. I think he can feel your feelings, though. So when you feel joy, he probably feels it too. But I don't know if he can see us. Do you think he can?"

"I hope so. He'd be so proud of me."

I recognize how strongly my son identifies himself with basketball so I decided to take the opportunity to help him think of himself as "special" for other reasons.

"Grandpa would be proud of your basketball skills, there's no question about that. But you do other things that would make him even more proud."

"Like what?"

"Remember the 7th grader that your buddies were teasing when I took you to school for registration? You walked up to them, looked at the younger boy and said, 'Don't worry kid; I won't let them throw you in a locker.' Your friends laughed and the younger kid beamed. Grandpa would've loved that."

Matt smiled and said, "That was Cody's little brother. They're always picking on him. He's used to it."

"Maybe he is, but the expression on his face said he was grateful for the intervention. And how about the way you always shake the hands of the referees after a game? Nobody else does that and sometimes you have to chase after them to do it. Why do you bother?"

"I don't know, it's a respect thing. Everyone yells at them all the time. I think it's a hard job."

"Trust me Matt, Grandpa is dancing in heaven over that kind of behavior. When you do your best and when you think beyond your own two feet, you always make him proud."

He rolled back onto his stomach, signaling to me that he'd love it if I started rubbing his back again. So I did. After a few minutes he added, "I wish I could talk to him."

"You can."

"No, I can't"

"Sure you can. You're connected through your hearts, so when you get ready to fall asleep just take a few deep breaths, close your eyes and try to completely relax. Then start the conversation in your head. It's not like you'll hear Grandpa's voice, but you'll know he's listening and he'll send you ideas. In the morning, when you wake up, you'll sort of feel like he gave you a hug."

With his eyes closed, Matt asked, "Seriously?"

"Hey, it works for me. Grandpa's your guardian angel. That means he's always listening."

"Ok, I'll try it…Love you."

"Sweet dreams baby," I added, kissing him on the cheek again.

I am humbled by the privilege of parenthood and recognize the influence I have on my children. Even in these technology-driven times, we are still the glue that holds our kids together and builds their foundation. We plant the seeds that become self-esteem by affirming them and noticing the things they do well, by teaching them responsibility and respecting their unique voice, and by supporting their highs and lows with unwavering love.

That foundation is critical to their success because there is no end to the challenges they will face in life. However, if they learn to stay in control of the ball, their problems will never define who they are. Hopefully their challenges will simply turn into something that they dribble around as they drive in to the basket and score.

✫ ✫ ✫

I'm still a consultant at ILS. Most of the work we do is leadership-related and the more time I spend with the leaders of various companies, the more I recognize some similarities among the best. Great leaders, it turns out, have three things in common. They treat everyone with respect. They are driven to do their best. And they do the right thing just because it's the right thing to do. The same three rules my parents taught me as a child apply in the workplace. The third rule is the most critical in business because leaders who do the right thing just because it's the right thing to do have the most influence.

It's one thing to do the right thing for a specific purpose, like increasing employee retention or meeting quarterly goals. It's another thing altogether to do the right thing just because it represents who you are and what you believe. Leaders in this second group are more genuine. They care about their employees and empower them to succeed. They build relationships, welcome feedback and take initiative. As a result, their employees trust them. They have influence because they've earned it by serving the people who choose to be part of their vision. These leaders are exceptional and their companies are great places to work.

I love coming in contact with centered leaders and realize that working with ILS has helped to reinforce the changes I've made in my life. Like, for instance, the time I was at an off-site with Steve and he had a group of twenty managers do an exercise called, "You, Inc." He had them create mission, vision, and values statements for their professional lives. The experience was powerful for many of them, just like it was for me when I created a mission statement for my personal life.

There's a famous line in *The Alchemist*. An old man is advising the shepherd boy to pursue his personal destiny and says, "When you want something, all the universe conspires in helping you to achieve it." That's how I feel these days. I feel like the entire universe is conspiring to help me succeed.

I now own a condo. My boys live with me half of the time and are doing great. Matt is 6'7" and confident in eighth grade. The troubles he had earlier in life are gone but not forgotten. He's developed compassion for his struggling peers, remembering what it felt like when things were harder for him. He's ready for the next challenge.

Chad is maneuvering his way through sixth grade, learning important lessons about organization and time management. His passion is still reading and I'm constantly running him to the library for books. He recently informed me that the library allows you to take out seventy-two books at one time. Fortunately, he can't carry that many.

Gina is back in school, adding a Spanish major to her psychology degree. She's still with Ethan who adores her and who's looking more like a yacht all the time. However, she's thinking about spending a year studying or working in Chili. She says she'll go alone.

The transition from college life to the "real" world is challenging for a lot of kids. Gina has more questions than answers these days and it bothers her. I think we underestimate how hard this time of life can be for our children. It's their biggest transition to date. Even though college was a significant step it was still more of what our kids are used to: school. It's not too hard for most of them to wrap their arms around those four years and succeed. Post-college involves a whole new set of parameters. They want to get it right and are often a little afraid of getting it wrong. There are more unknowns in their lives than ever before. For some reason they think they should have the answers. I remind Gina that trying things is how she'll find the answers. When she shared the idea of going to Chili for a while, I offered some support.

"Bean, you have all the tools to succeed," I said. "You're bound to make mistakes along the way so don't worry about that, it's OK. I think it's great that you want to travel. I'd miss you like crazy but it'd teach you volumes."

"I'd worry about losing my friends and what if I don't come back?"

"Come on Gina, with the internet, it's a really small world. Your important friends will always be your friends. And if you don't come back, I guess I'll have to learn some Spanish. Besides, the only reason you wouldn't come back would be if you were crazy happy there, right?"

"Yeah, you're right," she replied and then added, "Mom, I'm starting to worry about whether or not Ethan is right for me."

"Why? What's going on?"

"Well, it's like I have to take care of him. He plays video games constantly. I know he loves me and I love him too but I'm starting to think he's not very motivated. I might be too driven for him and it worries me."

"Ok, Bean listen. Two things: First, I think you guys are dealing with the same problem only you're not handling it the same way. You're both college graduates but neither of you has a clear path, right?"

"Right."

"Neither of you knows exactly what you want to do. On the one hand you're handling it by moving forward and opening new doors but on the other hand, maybe Ethan is handling it by running to his Xbox. He's probably feeling a lot of stress. I'd be slow to judge him on that."

"Maybe," she conceded. "But Mom, he says he wants to be a gym teacher and he's back in school for that but I have to do everything for him. He always waits to the last minute and then I end up fixing things. He wouldn't even be in the right classes if I didn't help him."

"Well that brings me to the second thing: Are you thinking about going to Chili as an excuse to break up with Ethan?"

"No, that's not it. I can't use a Spanish major unless I'm fluent, really fluent. I want to be immersed. But it would give us some time to figure out life on our own. Sometimes I wonder if he's doing what he's doing just to please me."

"Hmm, well you've got this year to work through the whole thing. I'm impressed that you can look at it so objectively. Honestly honey, I don't think I could do that at your age."

"Thanks Mom."

"Try to remember that you are only responsible for you. I think you'll both figure it out in the end."

"Yeah, sometimes I just wish I could see the future."

"No you don't," I said, laughing. "That would take all the adventure out of it. Besides, you can already see part of your future. You know you're back in school for one more year. By the time the year is over you will be ready for what's next. Just enjoy this time in your life, it'll be great."

"OK," she replied, slightly unsure.

"Gina," I said. "You're in charge of your direction. You understand that so you're way ahead of the game. It's all good."

"Thanks Mom."

Sometimes when I talk to her, I'm reminding myself how to live.

CHAPTER 14

We define ourselves by the best that is in us, not by the worst that has been done to us.
— EDWARD LEWIS

A work in progress

When Gina was three and frustrated about something, she'd put her hands on her hips and exclaim, "You are *not* the boss of me!" I'd laugh. Her determination sounded funny coming from such a small person. But, those words were really precious. They were the little voice of confidence guiding her. She dreamed big and believed she could do anything. Her words were the beginnings of self-esteem. She wanted to have control of her life.

We all know that three-year-olds don't have the judgment to make their own decisions. That would be ridiculous. So we teach them that they cannot be the boss. Mom is the boss. Dad is the boss. The teacher is the boss. While cruising through childhood, we teach them how to conform, how to follow the rules, how to meet expectations. If we're not careful, we end up teaching them to be compliant. They move from dreaming big to settling for the status quo. So much time is spent trying to please everyone else that our children can lose the little voice inside that wants control and if that happens, they become dependent on external sources for validation. Then everything they believe about themselves becomes a reflection of the opinions of the people around them. By the time they are adults, they're so used to this pattern that they settle into it for the rest of their lives.

I used to wonder what would have become of me if some key events hadn't occurred. What if my mother didn't come to Florida, assess my situation with Dick and step in to change it? What if I wasn't pushed to get a job and consequently didn't meet the cycling friends who initiated so many positive changes in my life? What if I didn't go to Nationals in St Louis, which led to Australia and France and Ironman? Without those events, would I have ever regained my self-esteem?

The answers don't matter. The journey matters. The events keep coming. They keep coming in your life and in mine. We have to embrace them and realize that they're critical pieces of the puzzle. Those difficult and sometimes painful events can be opportunities in disguise. Learning to work through challenging experiences helps to center us.

The unhappily-ever-after days are behind me, but that's not to say my life is a fairytale. No, I'm a work in progress and always will be. The biggest difference now is that I'm in charge of the progress. I've learned how to say "No." Of course I prefer to say, "Yes" but also realize it's foolish to try to please all of the people all of the time. I've learned that moving forward happens when we take care of ourselves from the inside out.

Sometimes my life is easy, sometimes it's hard. I'm usually happy but struggle with sadness now and then. It's OK. I've learned that the happiness I experience today is enhanced by the challenges of yesterday so I don't expect the journey to be easy. I just expect to keep moving forward. The idea is to make mistakes and learn from them. Then make more mistakes, just not the same ones, all the while gaining wisdom. The ups and downs are checks and balances; they keep us focused on the things that are important, the things we value the most. It doesn't matter what gets thrown in my path these days because I'm confident that I can handle it. I love the life I'm living.

Looking back, I recognize how lucky I've been. My brothers and I had parents who gave us guidelines but who didn't try to mold us into any particular thing. They respected us in the same way that they expected us to respect others. I've been loved and supported by my family throughout my life but I've also been loved and supported by countless friends. Maybe the angels I prayed to while sitting up in the bell tower of my church all those years ago were listening after all.

Success isn't about money or careers or relationships. Success is about knowing your 'self' and taking care of your 'self' before taking care of anyone else. Knowing your 'self' is the key to doing the right things in life. That feeling my mom always talked about, that feeling that comes from within, is joy. Success is about finding joy in the process of living.

Success doesn't come from steering your way through life, either. You have to drive. Chart a course, grab the wheel with both hands, and step on the gas. Make your life happen. If you have to navigate some icy patches or steer around a few roadblocks on the way to your destination, all the better, it'll make you a better driver.

There are numerous examples of centered people throughout history, people we can learn from, people who had passion for the things they believed in. They were driven to make a difference. Abraham Lincoln, Mahatma Gandhi, Martin Luther King, Jr., and Audrey Hepburn come to mind. They had influence because they were confident that they were doing the right things with their lives. And they were doing them just because they were the right things to do, not for recognition and certainly not to win the approval of others. These people also had an endless ability to stay the course. The more they gave, the more they had to give.

That's not to say that those incredibly inspiring people were perfectly centered. No, that kind of perfection resides only in God. But the more we grow in understanding of ourselves, our values and who we are from the inside out, the more centered we become.

So pay attention to the influences in your life, communicate, take care of your soul, forgive, and expect life to be challenging. Then add a heavy dose of fun, and you'll have something that's better than good.

This isn't the end of my story...it's just the beginning because I finally woke up and learned how to drive.

Epilogue

I'm traveling more now than ever before, mostly to speak. I speak to women's groups on a regular basis but also love challenging how high school and college students think about the value of their lives. With younger audiences I use the basketball analogy, building on the idea that they should be point guards. I want them to see their lives as an exciting journey that's worthy of big dreams no matter what kind adversity they have to dribble around as they drive into the basket and score.

Regardless of whether the group I'm fortunate enough to interact with is old or young, I try to leave a little time at the end for questions. What follows are some of the most frequently asked questions:

Q: You say the adversity in our lives makes us better people. Do you ever wonder what your life would have been like without some of the bad things that happened?

Yes. I struggled with that question for many years, especially in regard to the assault. For a long time I thought I'd give up everything, even if it meant I wouldn't have any of the same friends, even if it meant I wouldn't have my children. I hated the memory so much that I believed I would've given up the things I love the most for the chance to start over. In retrospect I realize that I shouldn't have done that to myself. Those feelings are called regret. Regret is a burden we shouldn't walk around with. Let me tell you a little story that illustrates this point.

When I was a kid, I was on a road trip with my family. We were on a freeway playing the license plate game when suddenly our car started making the scariest thumping sound. We had a flat tire. My dad managed to weave through the traffic, pulling us safely to the side of the road. Then he had to change the tire. All of us lamented about how unfortunate we were, not just because of the flat but because it was raining. Once back on the road, we made it maybe five miles before we found ourselves in a traffic jam, more bad luck. However, as we inched past the six car pileup, my mother noticed one of the license plates. It was the car in front of us when we got the flat tire. Immediately we all realized our good fortune.

I don't wonder about what might have been anymore. Maybe the other version of my life would have been great, maybe not. I don't care because this version is spectacular. Besides, I doubt I'd have the same passion moving forward without all the lessons of yesterday in my back pocket.

Q: Do you think people have to have adversity to live a great life?

I'm not sure how to answer that because I've never met anyone who's avoided adversity completely. However, I don't think it's handed out to us in equal portions and I don't think you have to experience personal tragedy to live an amazing life. But maybe personal tragedy helps you appreciate your amazing life. I also think you can learn vicariously from the mistakes other people make and avoid a lot of heartache. For example, I don't think any of you ever needs to experience the problems that come from getting arrested for driving under the influence. I hope you love yourselves and the other innocent people on the road enough to call a cab, just because it's the right thing to do, right? We'd be nuts if we went looking for adversity hoping it would make us better people. But when challenges cross our path, big or small, they teach us valuable lessons about ourselves and give us the kind of perspective that has the potential to make us better people.

Q: Isn't there such a thing as living a charmed life?

Yes. I've lived a charmed life. I bet you didn't see that coming, right? But I have; I have great parents, amazing friends, and wonderful children. Hell, I did an Ironman, how charmed is that! When you love the life you're living, when you feel lucky, when you wouldn't trade your life for anyone else's, you're living a charmed life. If we think about it globally, we should all feel charmed because we were lucky enough to be born in a country that values our freedom.

Q: Do you believe in destiny?

Sort of. Sometimes I think we get caught up in the idea that it doesn't matter what we do in life because our destiny is pre-set, right? Well, I think that's kind of an insult to God. There's a reason we constantly face choices. We're supposed to learn to choose well. We learn by trial and error, and we should get better at it with experience. The more often we choose to do the right thing just because it's the right thing to do, the closer we get to our destiny. Remember, you're the point guard. You have to decide what shots you're going to take. God won't take the shots for you. However, he owns the franchise and cheers louder than anyone else when you score.

Q: Did your father treat you differently after he found out?

Yes. He loved me more. I was more precious in his eyes. Parents are great that way. They love us unconditionally. The fear I had about talking to my parents, about disappointing them was incredibly misdirected. My greatest mistake was choosing not to talk. However, I also recognize that not everyone has parents who would support them in the same way. If tragedy strikes your life and you honestly believe talking to your parents would be a bad thing, you have to find an adult you can trust. Find a teacher or a counselor or someone from church or the parent of a friend, but find someone, someone safe, and then talk. You need perspective if you want to get back on track quickly. You're far too precious to waste a single day struggling with adversity all by yourself.

Q: I think it's brave that you tell your mistakes to help other people but don't you worry about what they'll think about you?

No. But I used to worry a lot. I've learned that I'm not the mistakes I made. Those things don't define me. What other people think doesn't define me either. What defines me is how much I value myself; how much I love myself; how connected I am to my soul. You shouldn't worry about the way other people think about you either. When something bad happens, you feel like every time kids see you they're thinking, "Awe, poor girl, that terrible thing happened to her." When you pass people in the hallway you think they're saying to their friends, "Isn't it terrible what happened to her. She must be a mess." Am I right?

OK, there could be some of that initially but it quickly dissipates. Honestly, before you know it, everyone is back to thinking about the usual critical news like who likes them and what they're doing after school. In their eyes you quickly revert back to the same person they've always known.

Q: What if I have absolutely no idea what I want to do with my life, what then?

The fact that you're asking me that question tells me you're going to figure it out. When I was your age I thought I was going to be a pharmacist. I changed majors so many times in college that I drove my parents crazy. Here's the thing, you just have to keep moving forward. The smartest thing you can do is get good grades because good grades open more doors. Lots of kids graduate from college still not knowing what they want to do. However, by then they have a lot more things on the list that they know they don't want to do. If you keep moving forward, doors keep opening and eventually you'll find something you love. When you do, chase it with everything you are.

Q: Did your parents do the same bedtime routine with you?

No. They'd send us upstairs to brush our teeth and get ready for bed and then we'd come back down for hugs and kisses. Then my mom would say, "Sweet dreams, I love you, may God bless you." That was it. We'd head back upstairs to bed.

However, my brothers and I had a lot of parent time because there were fewer things competing for our attention. We had dial telephones that were connected to the wall, no computers, one television, and no video games. We always ate dinner as a family and it was an event. Dinner time was catching up time. It was the time of day we filled Dad in on everything that happened. But I think my mom's favorite thing was after school snack time. It was her chance to gauge our day and impart some words of wisdom, whether we wanted them or not.

The bedtime routine I have with my kids is a byproduct of the busy lives we lead. After school activities are an everyday thing between sports and music lessons so I have to carve out one-on-one time with my children. For me, car-time and bedtime are equally priceless but very different. We often have the tough discussions in the car, saving bedtime for love and affirmation.

Q: What made the biggest impact in your life?

Well, clearly the rape. It was a life changing event for me, impacting my decision-making for over 30 years. If I handled it differently it might not have been so huge because I was blessed with such a great support system. But what good is a great support system if you don't take advantage of it? In hindsight I can see that I was on a giant detour. I was trying to move forward. I believed in those rules my parents instilled in me. I looked fine to the world too, but I lost my self-esteem that day. The good news, the important news is that I found it again. It reminds me of a George Eliot quote: "It's never too late to be who you might have been."

Q: What's next for you? Do you still compete? Will you write another book?

I'm still training because I like the discipline of fitness. I often come up with my best ideas when I'm out running in the woods. Exercise is a gift I give myself. I do plan to compete again as soon as the ability to train at a high level fits in with the other priorities in my life. As Stephen Covey would say we have to put first things first.

As for writing another book, yes, it's inevitable. I learned from writing *Wake Up* that I love to write. There were several times during the writing process when I'd take a detour, pouring out pages that were completely off track. I had to re-focus and remember what I was trying to accomplish. Some of those detours will become books. I think the first will address more directly the challenges of parenting through adversity. Then maybe I'll write a novel about a teenager trying to feel ok in the world.

Q: Did you ever think you'd be doing this?

Speaking? No. I never did. The thought never once crossed my mind that I'd do a triathlon, that I'd be a professional speaker, or that I'd write a book. That's what's so exciting about life. Sometimes it seems like everything is going wrong and then you find out that all of the hard times resulted in everything going right. We get this one chance to live a life that matters, that makes a difference. I think we have to embrace the whole of it, good and bad, in order to be great, really great.

About the Author

Wendy Naarup owns Tri and Tri Again LLC and is a principal consultant for Innovative Learning Strategies LLC, a leadership consulting firm located in Appleton, Wisconsin. She speaks to college students, high school students and women's groups about the bright side of adversity and taking control of their lives. She can be reached online at www.wendynaarup.com or at 920 427-1419.

Doing the right thing just because...

No matter how large or small, no matter how rural or urban, no community is immune from sexual assault and abuse. The numbers are staggering by any reasonable standard.

Because of the statistics that follow, 100% of the net profit from this book are donated to sexual assault crisis centers for education and prevention. Thank you for your support.

Sexual Assault Statistics
1 in 4 girls and 1 in 6 boys will be sexually assaulted by age 18.

- Finkelhor, David, et al. "Sexual Abuse in a National Survey of Adult Men and Women: Prevalence, Characteristics, and Risk Factors." 1990.

1 in 3 women around the world has been beaten, coerced into sex or otherwise abused during her lifetime.

- Heise, L., Ellsberg, M. and Gottemoeller, M. *Ending Violence Against Women. Population Reports, Series L, No. 11.*, December 1999
- Vlachovà, Marie and Biason, Lea, Eds. (2004) *Women in an Insecure World: Violence Against Women - Facts, Figures and Analysis.* Geneva Centre for the Democratic Control of Armed Forces.

Over 60% of sexual assault crimes go unreported
- U.S. Department of Justice.2005 National Crime Victimization Study. 2005.

For additional donations contact: www.sacc-**foxcities**.org or www.rainn.org

Made in the USA
Charleston, SC
18 June 2011